The Big Book of Instant Activities

HOW TO MAKE CLEAN COPIES FROM THIS BOOK

You may make copies of portions of this book with a clean conscience if

- you (or someone in your organization) are the original purchaser;
- you are using the copies you make for a noncommercial purpose (such as teaching or promoting your ministry) within your church or organization;
- you follow the instructions provided in this book.

However, it is ILLEGAL for you to make copies if

- you are using the material to promote, advertise or sell a product or service other than for ministry fund-raising;
- you are using the material in or on a product for sale; or
- you or your organization are not the original purchaser of this book.

By following these guidelines you help us keep our products affordable.
Thank you,
Gospel Light

Editorial Staff

Publisher, William T. Greig
Senior Consulting Publisher, Dr. Elmer L. Towns
Publisher, Research, Planning and Development, Billie Baptiste
Managing Editor, Lynnette Pennings, M.A.
Senior Consulting Editor, Wesley Haystead, M.S.Ed.
Senior Editor, Biblical and Theological Issues, Bayard Taylor, M.Div.
Senior Advisor, Biblical and Theological Issues, Dr. Gary S. Greig
Senior Editor, Sheryl Haystead
Editor, Margaret Self
Contributing Editors, Mandy Abbas, Anne Arneson, Mary Gross, Linda Mattia, Carol Niblette, Jay Bea Summerfield
Contributing Writers, Vicki Johnson, Rebecca Kortan, Lois Morgan, Becky Rowe, Katrina Steiner
Illustrator, Chizuko Yasuda
Designer, Zelle Olson

How to Use this Book

WHAT are Instant Activities?

Just what the name says: activities you can use at once. Most require NO preparation. Some require only a small bit of preparation, using materials you have at hand (such as paper and markers). Read the brief, easy-to-follow instructions and you and your children will be ready for fun.

WHO are Instant Activities planned for?

Those people who guide young children (three years and up) at

- Sunday School
- Children's Church
- Vacation Bible School
- Day school
- Child care
- Home
- Preschool
- Kindergarten
- Birthday parties
- Outdoor facilities (park, playground)
- Places where children must sit quietly and wait (at a doctor's office, in a car, in a shopping cart, etc.)

WHY use Instant Activities?

Movement, challenge and fun. Children are here-and-now people, and these activities involve children immediately. Each child may not join you right away in singing or repeating a rhyme, for example, but every child can mirror your motions at once.

All children need to move—often. God designed children with built-in wiggles and squirms. Instant Activities use this pent-up energy in a controlled and enjoyable manner, pleasant for both children and adults.

Children enjoy the challenge of learning new skills and information—if these things are interesting and within each child's understanding and physical abilities. Instant Activities include a variety of opportunities for children to learn through their God-given senses: hearing, seeing, touching, tasting.

Here's the best part of Instant Activities from the children's viewpoint: The activities are FUN! Enjoy these activities with the children you guide. Add a smile to your words. If you're happy and enthusiastic, then the children will reflect your joy.

Contents

Circle Time Activities...15

The brief attention spans of young children can make it challenging to keep minds and bodies from wandering off during group time. Circle time activities can quickly recapture interest and allow wiggly bodies to move appropriately.

Cleanup Activities...27

Encouraging children to participate in cleanup tasks helps children learn responsibility and develops childrens' sense of accomplishment. Cleanup activities motivate children to work together to care for their room and materials.

Finger Play Activities...37

Finger plays appeal to a child's imagination and sense of rhythm. The finger plays in this book will provide a welcome change of pace in a session for young children. Repeat finger plays often, so children become familiar with them.

Activity Finger Plays

Get-Acquainted Activities . . . 63

What is the most welcome sound to a child's ears? His or her name! Get-acquainted activities provide opportunities for children to respond to their names and to learn the names of others in the group. These experiences help each child to feel that he or she belongs—that *this* is a place where he or she is loved, valued and accepted.

Movement Activities...75

Young children are physically active and need plenty of opportunities for movement of their whole bodies. Movement activities require open space, indoors or outdoors, so children can enjoy expending their energy as they develop large motor skills.

Music Activities...89

Music and rhythm activities help regain wandering attention faster than almost anything else! Young children are attracted to music and movement, even if they don't always sing along. Using music activities can also boost the group's joy factor by leaps and bounds!

Quiet Activities...107

Quiet activities provide children with a welcome change of pace when they need a break from active involvement. Children will enjoy quiet activities individually or in small groups.

Transition Activities...127

Children are not always ready to move from one activity to another when the schedule says it's time. Transition activities help with those changes. They assist in bringing conclusion to a previous activity and they make the first step in moving to the next one.

Word Activities...147

for Older Children

Take advantage of children's interest in learning to read by leading them in a variety of language activities. Written especially for older children, word activities encourage children to practice and expand their vocabulary.

Age-Level Characteristics of Young Children

2s and 3s

Physical

From two to three years the child is in constant movement. The child tumbles often. Large muscles are developing, but small hand/finger muscles are not developed. Twos walk, climb, scribble on paper, build a tower with blocks, turn pages of a book and feed themselves snacks. Threes may build structures with blocks, draw pictures which they will name as objects/people, begin to count and may begin to use scissors on heavy straight lines.

Teaching Tips: Plan for freedom of movement. Use simple finger play and activity songs for stretching, stepping, jumping and clapping. Also provide some quiet-time activities.

Mental/Emotional

Twos have short attention spans. They may say many single words and some sentences. The child is beginning to recognize his or her name in print. Two- and three-year-olds are explorers; they learn through their senses. They can learn rhymes, songs and finger plays.

Teaching Tips: Provide materials with interesting textures, smells, tastes, etc. for children to explore. Use literal, simple language with no symbolism. Be brief and often use pictures. When telling children what to do, give one brief direction at a time. Wait patiently until they have responded before you continue with the next direction.

Social

Twos have little regard for the rights of others. Threes can interact in play with others. However, it's still a "ME, MY, MINE" world. Sharing and taking turns is hard to do. When a conflict arises, children respond better to distraction than to reasoning.

Teaching Tips: Kindness and patience are necessary. Offer opportunities for play with other children. Know each child as an individual and use his or her name often. Help each child to succeed by providing activities appropriate for the child's abilities.

Spiritual

The two- and three-year-old can learn that God made all things and that God cares for him or her; that Jesus is God's special Son and that He did kind, loving things when He lived on Earth; that the Bible is a special book about God and Jesus and that Bible stories are true.

Teaching Tips: The child's learning about God is dependent on not only what people say but also what people show about God. Your loving actions help the child understand God's love. Help the child experience God's presence in our world through a variety of seeing, touching, smelling, tasting and hearing activities. Talk and sing about God.

4s and 5s

Physical

At this age children are in a period of rapid physical growth. Coordination is greatly improved. These children are still constantly on the move—running, jumping, walking or climbing—and need open spaces to move about freely! Girls often mature more rapidly than boys.

Teaching Tips: Because children at this age are gaining control of small muscles, provide activities that involve fine coordination. The rapid growth and constant activity of the child causes easy fatigue, so alternate times of active and quiet activity.

Mental/Emotional

Fours and fives are curious and questioning. They may concentrate for longer periods, but their attention span is still short. Children will interpret your words literally. Fours and fives may talk accurately about recent events and pronounce most common words correctly.

Teaching Tips: Use large teaching pictures to reinforce basic concepts. Set realistic limits and emphasize the behavior you desire. ("Ryan, running is a good thing to do outside where there is lots of room. Inside we have to walk, so no one will get hurt." "Chantel, you may only draw on your own paper. Are there any more places on your page that you want to make purple?") Supply a variety of materials for children to touch, see, smell and taste. Help children discover things for themselves by having the freedom to experiment (play) with a variety of safe materials.

Social

The four- or five-year-old child can participate with other children in group activities. The child actively seeks adult approval, responds to friendliness and wants to be loved, especially by his or her teacher. Some children may use negative ways of gaining attention from others.

Teaching Tips: Provide opportunities for group singing and conversation. Give each child individual attention before negative behavior occurs. Make eye contact often, listen carefully to the child and smile and show that the child is special to you.

Spiritual

The four- and five-year-old child can learn basic information about God—He made the world; He cares for all people; He forgives him or her when the child is sorry for doing wrong. A child this age can also learn that Jesus died to take the punishment for the wrong things we have done and that He rose from the dead and is alive. Fours and fives can be taught that the Bible tells us ways to obey God and that he or she can talk to God in prayer.

Teaching Tips: Because the child still thinks literally and physically, avoid the use of symbolic words and phrases such as "born again," "open your heart" or "fishers of men." When about to use a symbolic expression, think of the simplest literal explanation you could give of what the expression means. Then use that simple explanation *instead* of the symbolic one, which may confuse the child.

Classroom Discipline Tips

"What a morning this has been!" comments a bewildered teacher.

"Why can't little children sit still?" sighs another. "What these kids need is discipline!"

Why is a child's behavior sometimes puzzling and frustrating? Why *do* children "act like that"?

No two children are alike. We cannot begin to number the different experiences each child has had in the first six years of life. Nor can we fathom the varying expectations that families have placed upon these children. And yet—knowing these things—we continue to be surprised when children do not act the way we have anticipated they will act.

By the same token, no two teachers are alike. And yet most of us, when surrounded by a roomful of children, are painfully alike. We want children to *behave*—which usually means we want them to act the way we anticipate they will act!

Where can the weary teacher find help? Is discipline the answer? And just what *is* discipline?

Allow Freedom Within Limits

Good discipline is what you do *with* and *for* a child, not what you do *to* him or her. Discipline, then, is the guidance an adult gives so that a child knows what he or she *may* do as well as what he or she *may not* do.

For a child to grow into a thoughtful and loving adult, he or she needs to begin developing self-control—direction from within. To accomplish this lifelong task, the child needs loving and understanding adults to guide behavior until he or she is mature enough to handle the task alone.

Learning to get along with others and to creatively use materials and equipment help a child enjoy the beginning of his or her church school experience. A child has (we hope) many years of church attendance ahead. How important, then, that these first experiences be pleasant ones! To establish a positive learning atmosphere, there are three important points to remember.

Provide love and care for each child. This love is not the gushy kind but a love that gives a child what he or she needs to grow and develop. Children long to feel that someone cares about them, that they are people of worth and value. Demonstrate your love and care in ways a child can understand. Sit down at the child's eye level and listen attentively to what a child has to say. Kindly but firmly redirect a child's out-of-bounds activity. When you redirect a child's disruptive or unacceptable activity, do not scold or shame the child. Scolding or shaming makes the child feel excluded from your love. Focus on the child's *behavior,* not on the person. Let the child know you love him or her but that you cannot allow the misbehavior. In all your actions and words, reflect the unconditional love you yourself have experienced from God.

Plan an interesting schedule of activities. If you expect children to sit quietly and "wait for an activity to begin," then you are asking them to act like miniature adults. Normal young children often misbehave simply because they are bored. Young children need action. As they grow and learn, they *must* move around. They learn best by touching and testing everything around them. For this reason, it's best to offer a variety of activities.

Help children feel a sense of security and order. Tell them by your actions and your words that they are safe in your care and that you will allow no harm to come to them. Children also find security in knowing you are nearby to assist when they need help. When they are assured you will be there to help, they will be more willing to try a new activity or experience.

Children like to be fairly sure of what will happen next. Follow the same schedule of activities each week. Of course, there will be times when you will need to be flexible by shortening or lengthening parts of the schedule, depending on the interest and attention span of the children.

A child feels secure with limits. He or she needs to know what you expect. Establish a few basic rules such as "Dough stays on the table." Phrase the rules in a positive way whenever you can. Help children remember and observe the rules during their work and play. Give each child consistent and positive guidance. Find a middle ground between rigid authority and total permissiveness. Children need limits; but they also need freedom to move around and make choices within those limits.

Children respond in a positive way to a neatly arranged room with fresh and interesting things to do. The same old stuff in the same old places, with pieces missing or parts broken, is almost certain to invite misbehavior.

When a child receives an adult's thoughtful and consistent guidance, he or she is on the way to understanding what it means to be responsible for one's own behavior. From this responsibility grows self-control—discipline from within.

Control Unacceptable Behavior

Sometimes a teacher's most thoughtful preparation and guidance does not keep a child from misbehaving. With most preschoolers, you have only about 10 seconds to do the correcting. Avoid long explanations. Although there are no surefire guarantees for these special situations, here are brief suggestions to guide you:

When a child hits (kicks, scratches)—"That hurts. I cannot let you hit Shannon. And I cannot let Shannon hit you. You may not hurt other people here. *Tell* Shannon what you want." Separate the two children. Redirect the offender's activity to another area of the room, and stay with the child until he or she is constructively involved.

When a child bites—"Biting hurts. We use our teeth only to chew food." Never encourage a child to bite back to "show how it feels."

When a child spits—"Your spit belongs in your mouth. If you need to spit, you may spit in the toilet."

When a child uses offensive names—"Do not call Alex stupid. He is not stupid. He is drawing the way he thinks is best. Alex is doing a good job of drawing. And you are doing a good job of drawing."

When a child has a tantrum—This is no time for words. The child is too upset to listen. Hold the child firmly until he or she calms down. When you hold the child, you are offering protection as well as control. If other children are frightened by the tantrum, take the child to another room with an adult to supervise. Explain to children, "Katie is having trouble now. She will be all right in a little while."

Redirect Distracting Behavior

Activity does not prevent a child from listening or learning. When a child's activeness is not interfering with another child's attention, let that child do what his or her energy is requiring at that time. However, there are some general guidelines that can help limit distractions during large group times.

If a child's activity is interfering with another child, signal a teacher or helper to sit beside or behind the active child. The teacher can gently guide arms and legs back into the active child's own space or provide a productive alternate activity the child can do. ("Timmy, if you want to stay here next to John, you must keep your hands in your own lap. Or would you rather come and look at a book?")

Simply state what the child is to do with his or her hands. It is often appropriate to tell the child what will happen if he or she continues to disturb (e.g, be moved to another place).

If the disturbing actions continue, do *exactly* what you said you would do. Your effectiveness depends on your ability to follow through on your promise.

If more than one child is showing signs of restlessness, realize that it's time to do something else (e.g., an instant activity, sing a song, stand and stretch, etc.).

When a child consistently misbehaves during activities, remove the child from the scene of the difficulty. "Joshua, books are for looking at, not for tearing. We do not tear books. I have to put away the books." "Amy, you need to come to the puzzle table. I see the puzzle with horses on it that you like." Keep conversation cheerful.

Help the child handle negative feelings by accepting them. "Lupe, I know you feel angry at Jennifer for knocking down your blocks. But you may not hit Jennifer and Jennifer may not hit you."

Watch to determine what makes the child want to continue negative behavior. Sometimes misbehavior is simply a bid for attention. Quite often a child would rather be punished (which is one way to get adult attention) than receive no attention.

Avoid repeated threats. There is a difference between a threat ("Wesley, if you do that again, I will . . . ") and explaining consequences ("I cannot let you do that because it might hurt someone"). A threat is a form of a dare that increases tension, while an explanation of consequences (in terms a child can understand) defines limits.

Circle Time Activities

The brief attention spans of young children can make it challenging to keep minds and bodies from wandering off during group time. Circle time activities can quickly recapture interest and allow wiggly bodies to move appropriately.

All Eyes on Me!

Procedure: Children sit in a circle. Say,

One, two, three;
All eyes on me!

Children look at you carefully. **Now close your eyes.** Turn around and change one item of your appearance (remove a watch, put on glasses, add a sweater or scarf, etc.). At your signal, children open their eyes and try to guess what has changed. Repeat game, changing a different item of your appearance for each round.

Amazing Animal List

Materials: Large sheet of paper, marker.

Procedure: Show children the paper. **Let's think of the names of enough animals to fill this whole paper!** Children take turns naming animals. On sheet of paper, print name of each animal. Give hints if children have difficulty thinking of animals that have not already been named. **I'm thinking of an animal with a very long trunk.** Or make the sound of that animal.

Continue activity until paper is full. Then lead children in counting all the animal names on the paper.

Variation: Challenge children to fill up additional papers with other lists: names of people to show love to, favorite foods, names of colors, etc.

Animal Moves

Procedure: Invite a volunteer to call out the name of an animal. All children pretend to be the animal, moving and making sounds. Continue with other animals.

For Older Children: Children form pairs and decide on an animal to be and then practice moving like the animal. Each pair pantomimes animal for others to guess.

If the story of Noah and his family is familiar to children, choose one pair of children to be Noah and his wife and invite remaining children to be animals. Designate an area of the room to be the ark. Invite Noah and his wife to stand at the "entrance" to the ark. Animals line up and move like their chosen animal around the room and onto the ark. If time and interest allow, extend the activity by having children act out additional story events: the ark rocking in the storm, the raven and the dove flying out of the ark and back, and the animals getting off the ark and onto dry land.

Beach-Ball Roll

Materials: Beach ball.

Procedure: Children sit in a circle with feet stretched forward and legs apart. **I thank God for sunshine. Kim, what do you want to thank God for?** Roll the ball to Kim. She names something she wants to thank God for and rolls the ball to another child. Continue game until each child has had a turn to name something and roll the ball.

Variation: Substitute other responses for children to give, such as naming their favorite animals, colors, foods, etc.

Bible-Times Travel

Procedure: Jesus and His friends didn't have cars to ride in. Instead, they walked, rode in a boat or rode on a donkey. Let's pretend to travel like Jesus and His friends.

Ride your donkey. Lead children to walk, bouncing up and down as though riding a donkey. **Row your boat.** Children move their arms in a rowing motion as they walk. **Walk on the road.** Children walk.

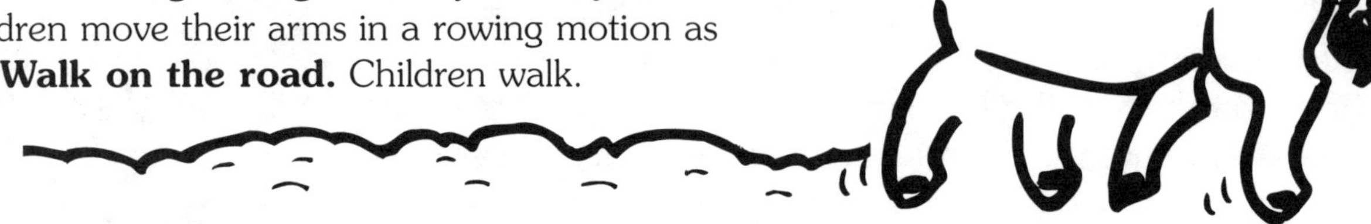

Color Code

Materials: Construction paper in three colors, scissors.

Preparation: Cut construction paper into strips, one for each child.

Procedure: Children sit in a circle. Give a paper strip to each child, varying the colors so that every third child has the same color of paper.

Call out a color and a way of moving (hopping, running, skipping, galloping, walking, crawling, etc.). Each child holding a paper of the color you named stands up and in the manner called, moves around the circle once and back to his or her place. Repeat activity, naming different colors and different ways of moving. Invite children to trade strips so that each child has a different color. Then repeat the activity.

For Older Children: Challenge children to play the game silently. Instead of calling out a color and a way of moving, stand in the middle of the circle, hold up a color of paper and demonstrate a way of moving. Without talking, children holding the matching color of paper stand up and move around the circle in the manner you demonstrated.

Color Matchup

Materials: Paper in a variety of colors, scissors.

Preparation: Cut paper into slips, one for each child; cut at least two slips of each color.

Procedure: Children sit in a circle. Give each child a slip of paper. **Find another person who has the same color of paper as you. Sit down by that person.** Children form pairs or groups.

When all children are seated, ask one pair or group, **What color paper do you have? What do you see in our room that is the same color? What is a fruit that is the same color?**

For Older Children: Lay a large sheet of white paper on the floor in the middle of the circle. One at a time, ask children to place their colored paper on the white paper, placing same colors in rows so that a graph is formed. Children count the number of each color and then tell which color has the most and the least slips.

Copycat Game

Procedure: Lead children in saying the following rhyme:

Let's play Copycat just for fun.
Let's copy Julie. She's the one.
Whatever she does, we'll do the same.
That's how we'll play the Copycat game.

Julie does a motion (jumps with both feet, touches head, pats legs, turns around, looks up and then down, hops on one foot, etc.). Children copy her. Julie points to the next child to be named in the activity.

Repeat until all children have been named and have demonstrated a motion for group to copy.

Feel for It

Materials: Large paper bag, a variety of objects (crayon, block, toy car, etc.).

Procedure: Secretly place one of the objects into the bag. **Without looking, put your hand in this bag and try to guess what is in it.** Children take turns to feel the object in the bag and guess what it is. After all children have had a turn, remove the object from the bag. Continue with other objects.

What else can you do with your hands beside feel things? (Draw. Throw a ball. Play computer games.)

Variation: Bring nature items (acorn, pinecone, bark, shell, rock, leaf, etc.) for children to feel and identify. Talk about each item's texture, size and color.

The Feeling Song

Procedure: Lead children in singing the following words to the tune of "If You're Happy and You Know It":

If you're happy and you know it,
Smile a smile. *(Smile.)*
If you're happy and you know it,
Smile a smile. *(Smile.)*
If you're happy and you know it,
Then your face will surely show it—
If you're happy and you know it,
Smile a smile. *(Smile.)*

What makes you feel happy? Volunteers respond.

Repeat with the following words and corresponding actions, asking about each emotion as you finish each verse:

1. **If you're angry and you know it, stomp your feet.**
2. **If you're sad and you know it, say boo-hoo.**
3. **If you're sleepy and you know it, give a yawn.**
4. **If you're silly and you know it, laugh out loud.**
5. **If you're scared and you know it, shake and shiver.**

Foot Fumble

Materials: One small object for each child (pencil, craft stick, crayon, toy car, etc.).

Procedure: Children sit in a circle. Place an object in the middle of the circle. Children remove shoe and sock from one foot. Each child has a turn to try to pick up the object using only his or her toes.

Variation: Children remove one of their shoes and place them in the middle of the circle. Choose a child to take a shoe from the pile and then move around the circle to find the child with the matching shoe. That child, in turn, takes a shoe from the pile and then finds the child with the matching shoe. Continue until all children have matching shoes.

God's Creation

Procedure: Begin the activity by naming something God made. **God made dolphins.** Move your hands like a dolphin. Children imitate your motion.

Volunteer names something God made and makes motion to represent the item. For example, a child who says "God made trees" could stand straight up with his or her hands spread out above his or her head. Other children imitate the action.

Extend the activity by continuing to talk about the item. **Now the wind is blowing very gently. The trees are slowly swaying in the wind. Now the wind is blowing very hard. The trees are bending in the wind.** Use appropriate motions for children to imitate. Continue as time and interest permit.

God's Garden

Procedure: Children stand in a circle. Choose one child to be the Farmer. Remaining children will be Seeds. As you lead all children in singing the following words to the tune of "The Farmer in the Dell," Farmer touches Seeds on the head. When they are touched, the Seeds curl up in a ball on the floor.

The farmer plants the seed.
The farmer plants the seed.
Hi-ho, the derry-o,
The farmer plants the seed.

Choose another child to be the Sun. As group sings, Sun forms a sun shape by holding his or her arms in a circle over his or her head and walks around "shining" on the Seeds.

The sun shines bright and warm.
The sun shines bright and warm.
Hi-ho, the derry-o,
The sun shines bright and warm.

Choose another child to be the Rain. As group sings, Rain walks around the circle "sprinkling" on the Seeds with his or her fingers.

God sends the rain.
God sends the rain.
Hi-ho, the derry-o,
God sends the rain.

As all children sing together, Seeds begin to stretch and wiggle.

The seeds begin to grow.
The seeds begin to grow.
Hi-ho, the derry-o,
The seeds begin to grow.

As all children sing together, Seeds stamp their feet on the ground.

The roots grow deep and strong.
The roots grow deep and strong.
Hi-ho, the derry-o,
The roots grown deep and strong.

As all children sing together, Seeds wave their arms above their heads.

The leaves grow tall and straight.
The leaves grow tall and straight.
Hi-ho, the derry-o,
The leaves grow tall and straight.

The Same Game

Procedure: Children sit in a circle, feet stretched toward the center. Say, **I see five children who are all wearing tennis shoes.** Children try to identify the five children. Continue game, varying the number and type of item that is the same (clothing colors, clothing types, hair bows, etc.).

For Older Children: Tell children you see a certain number of objects in the room that are the same (six red objects, three objects shaped like a circle, etc.). Children try to identify the objects.

Shape Sighting

Procedure: Children sit in a circle. **Look around our room to see something shaped like a circle.** Children look at toys, furniture, windows, doors, clock, etc. Call on volunteers to name what they see shaped like a circle. Repeat game, naming square, triangle and rectangle.

For Younger Children: Cut large shapes from paper to acquaint children with the shape before asking them to look for an identical shape.

For Older Children: Print a list of all the objects children name for each shape. Compare lists to find out which shape is most prevalent.

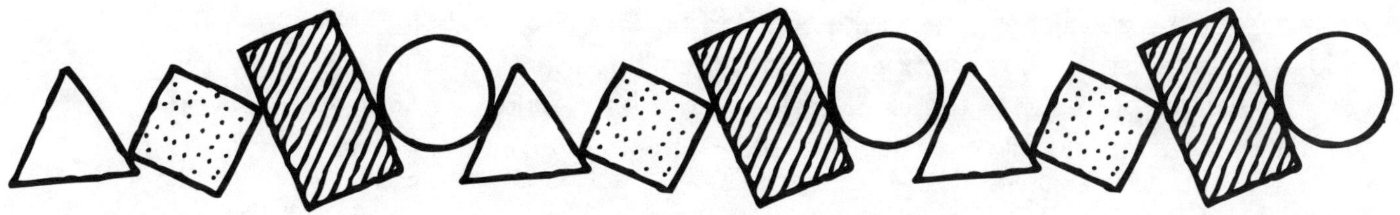

Sticker Search

Materials: A variety of stickers, two of each design.

Procedure: Give each child a sticker to put onto his or her shirt. (Optional: Place stickers on children.)

Find a friend who has the same sticker as you do. Each child looks for a child with a matching sticker. Children with matching stickers sit beside each other for the next activity.

What Do You See?

Materials: Cardboard tube; optional—pair of eyeglasses with no lenses.

Procedure: Children sit in a circle. Volunteer holds cardboard tube up to eye. (Optional: Volunteer puts on glasses.) Lead children in chanting to volunteer,

Nathan, Nathan,
What do you see?

Nathan responds,

I see (name of child sitting to left of him)
Looking at me!

Nathan gives the cardboard tube to the child on his left. That child looks through tube. Children chant first two lines of poem and then child responds by repeating the last two lines, using the name of the child on his or her left. Activity continues until everyone has had a turn and tube has been passed all the way around the circle.

For Older Children: Invite children to substitute the following phrases and actions for "looking at me": "waving at me," "frowning at me," "smiling at me," "laughing at me."

What Is Missing?

Materials: Bible story figures and a flannel board.

Procedure: After telling the Bible story, display all figures on flannel board. Ask children to close their eyes. Remove one of the figures from flannel board.

Open your eyes and see if you can tell which person from our story is missing! Children respond. **Karen and Will are right! It was Jesus. In our Bible story, what did Jesus do to help His friends?**

Put back the Jesus figure and repeat activity, removing a different figure. Continue playing game and reviewing story as children's interest allows.

Where Is Kyle?

Procedure: Children sit in a circle. **When you hear me sing your name, please stand up.** Demonstrate procedure and responses with a child. Lead children in singing these words to the tune of "Where Is Thumbkin?"

Where is Kyle?

Where is Kyle?

Here I am. Here I am. (Kyle stands and sings response.)

How are you today, Kyle?

Very well, I thank you. (Kyle sings this response.)

We're glad you're here.

We're glad you're here. (Kyle remains standing.)

Repeat until each child has been named and is standing.

Who Is Here Today?

Procedure: Children stand in a circle. Sing these words to the tune of "The Farmer in the Dell," using names of children. Clap as you sing.

Who is here today?
Who is here today?
Let's all clap our hands and see
Who is here today.

Heather's here today.
Ethan's here today.
Haydn, Jeff and Sabrina
They're all here today.

Each child sits down as you sing his or her name. Repeat song until all children have been named and are seated. Then sing,

We're all here today,
We're all here today,
Let's all clap together,
For we're all here today.

Cleanup Activities

Encouraging children to participate in cleanup tasks helps children learn responsibility and develops children's sense of accomplishment. Cleanup activities motivate children to work together to care for their room and materials.

Cleanup Song

Procedure: To guide cleanup activities, sing these words to the tune of "London Bridge Is Falling Down." Use a child's name and the activity he or she is do to.

Kristy can help stack the blocks,
Stack the blocks, stack the blocks.
Kristy can help stack the blocks.
Kristy is helping.

Continue with other children's names, using other appropriate phrases ("fix the puzzles," "wipe the table," "pick up scraps," etc.).

Finish the song with this verse:

Thank you, friends, for cleaning up,
Cleaning up, cleaning up.
Thank you, friends, for cleaning up.
Our room is clean!

Color Clean

Procedure: Assign cleanup jobs to children according to the dominant color of their clothing. **I see that Thomas and Logan are wearing green. You may put all the scissors in this basket.** Thomas and Logan begin their cleanup task. **I see that Jeremy and Amanda are wearing red. You may pick up the waste paper and put it in this wastepaper basket.** Continue naming children and their cleanup task. Be specific!

Counting Cleanup

Procedure: When children are putting away equipment containing many items (blocks, crayons, small toys, plastic building toys, etc.), say, **If you are five years old, you may put five cars on this shelf.** Or ask, **How many blocks do you think you can stack? Four? Six? Seven?** Children count along with you as they clean.

Do Your Share

Procedure: As children do cleanup tasks, say this rhyme:

Clean up, clean up,
Everybody, everywhere;
Clean up, clean up,
Everybody do your share.

Repeat the rhyme at short intervals throughout the activity. Vary the rhyme by saying it quickly, slowly, softly or loudly.

Helping Time

Procedure: Five minutes before beginning cleanup, say, **In a few minutes, you will need to stop your work.** After five minutes, begin singing the following words to the tune of "Jingle Bells":

Stopping time, stopping time—
It's time to stop your play.
Stopping time, stopping time—
We'll play another day.

Helping time, helping time—
It's helping time today.
Helping time, helping time—
Help put your dolls away.

Repeat song several times as you move about activity areas. With each repetition, insert the name of the objects children need to put away.

I Spy

Procedure: While children are cleaning the room, name different objects you notice that need to be put away. **I spy something blue by the block shelves. It's not a block.**

When a child finds it and puts it in its place, say, **Thank you, Brian for finding the blue car and putting it on the car shelf.** Repeat, naming other items that children haven't yet cleaned up. Be sure to commend those who see the items and put them away.

Masking-Tape Vacuums

Materials: Masking tape.

Preparation: Tear masking tape into 8-inch (20.5-cm) long strips, one for each child.

Procedure: When an art project or other activity has resulted in small scraps on the floor, turn the children into masking-tape vacuums. Wrap each child's hand with a strip of masking tape, sticky side out. Wrap the tape widthwise across the palm and around the back of the hand. Attach ends of tape so it stays over hand as a loop. Demonstrate how to pick up scraps so that they stick to the tape.

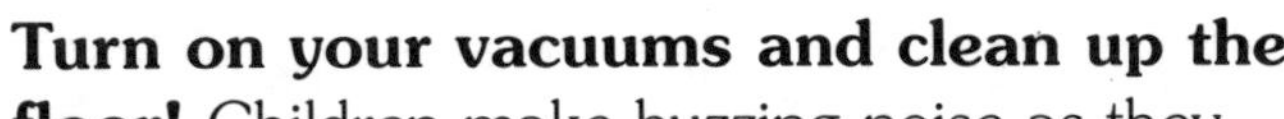

Turn on your vacuums and clean up the floor! Children make buzzing noise as they stick hands against scraps to collect them on the masking tape. When the floor is clean, invite children to turn off their vacuums and throw away their masking tape.

Now It's Time

Procedure: Sing these words to the tune of "Mary Had a Little Lamb" while all children clean the room:

Now it's time to stack the dishes,
Stack the dishes, stack the dishes.
Now it's time to stack the dishes,
Cleaning up is fun!

As you walk from one area to another, substitute words to reflect children's activity ("fix the puzzles," "throw away trash," "put away dolls," etc.).

Partner Cleanup

Procedure: Children form pairs by matching the first letter of their first names. Pairs work together to put away materials and equipment. Encourage cleanup by what you see. **I see Marcy and Michel putting scissors in the scissor box. I see Joel and Joshua putting away glue sticks. The people in our room really know how to clean up!**

Puppet Pal

Materials: Hand puppet.

Preparation: Give your puppet a name (Cleanup Kid, Carlee Cleanup, etc.).

Procedure: Use the puppet to announce cleanup time. Have the puppet make positive and encouraging comments to the children as they clean up the room. **Kelley and Jeffery have put lots of long blocks on the shelf. Lillian and Tina picked up every scrap of paper and put them in the waste basket. Good work!**

Quiet Cleanup

Procedure: Today we're going to play a game. We're going to clean up our room without making any sounds or using our voices. Listen while we work silently to hear other sounds we usually don't notice. Lead children in putting away materials and equipment as silently as possible. Show children how to mouth words to each other if communication is needed.

When children have finished, ask, **What are some things we can hear when we are quiet and don't talk?**

Robots to the Rescue

Procedure: What is a robot? Volunteer answers. **Show us how robots move. Let's practice moving stiffly like robots.** After children have gotten the idea, say, **We're going to pretend we are robots when we clean our room today!** Assign children specific cleanup tasks. **Ready? Robots clean!** Children move like robots to clean up assigned areas.

Singing Praises

Procedure: To direct attention to children who are modeling helpful cleanup behavior and to encourage children who are having difficulty cleaning up, sing these words to the tune of "Did You Ever See a Lassie?"

Adam is a helper, a helper, a helper.
Adam is helping put markers away.

Insert child's name and the task he or she is doing, repeating the song as many times as needed. Be sure to sing about any child who has improved after having had difficulty cleaning up.

Speedy Song

Materials: Children's music cassette/CD with a fast-paced song, cassette/CD player.

Procedure: After children have been assigned specific cleanup tasks, say, **I'm going to play some very fast music while we clean our room today. Let's try cleaning up as fast as the music goes. If we work quickly, we can probably finish before the music is over.**

Play the song again if children have not finished putting things away by the time the song ends the first time.

Time It!

Materials: Stopwatch or watch with a second hand.

Procedure: Before beginning cleanup activities, show children the watch and describe its purpose. Time children as they put away materials and equipment, calling out "Begin" when you start to keep track of the time. When the last item is put away, tell children the time on the watch. **You worked so quickly to clean our room today! I wonder how long it will take us the next time we clean up.**

You Choose!

Procedure: Before beginning cleanup activity, gather children in a circle. **Let's name the places in our room that we need to clean up.** Guide children to name activity areas (blocks, puzzles, home living, art table, etc.). **Think of what place you'd like to clean up. When you've decided, raise your hand.** Let children tell their preferences. Then assign areas. **Lydia and Annie have decided to put away our markers and scissors. Jason, Morgan and Jon have decided to stack the carpet squares.** Continue until all children are involved in cleanup tasks.

Finger Play Activities

Finger plays appeal to a child's imagination and sense of rhythm. The finger plays in this book will provide a welcome change of pace in a session for young children. Repeat finger plays often, so children become familiar with them.

shh!

Grab Your Knees

Grab your knees, touch your toes.

Turn around, and put your finger on your nose.

Flap your arms, jump up high,

Wiggle your fingers, and reach for the sky.

I Clap My Hands

I clap my hands, I touch my feet,

I jump up from the ground.

I clap my hands, I touch my feet

And turn myself around.

I clap my hands, I touch my feet,

I do not make a sound. Shhh!

I Have Ten Fingers

I have ten fingers

And they all belong to me.

I can make them do things—

Would you like to see?

I can shut them up tight,

I can open them wide,

I can put them together,

I can make them all hide,

I can make them jump high,

I can make them jump low,

I can fold them so quietly

And hold them just so.

I Sit Down

I sit down, then stand up and clap both my hands.

I put my foot forward and right back again.

I raise my arms high, and clap both my hands.

I stand up quite tall, and I sit down again.

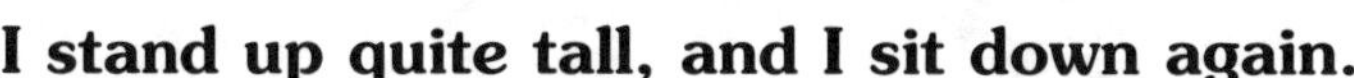

I sit very straight with both feet on the floor.

I fold my hands this way and look at the door.

I look at the ceiling; I look at the wall.

I look at my teacher and stand up quite tall.

I Stand Up Tall

I stand up tall and turn around

And jump, jump, jump!

I stand up tall and clap my hands

With a thump, thump, thump!

I stand up tall and reach up high,

Then clap, clap, clap!

I stand up tall then bend down low

And clap, clap, clap!

I Stretch

I stretch and stretch and find it fun

To reach and try to touch the sun.

I bend and bend to touch the floor

'Til muscles in my legs get sore.

I stretch and try to reach the sky,

To touch the stars as they go by.

I bend so I can touch my toes,

Then straighten up and touch my nose.

I'll Touch

I'll touch my head,

My hair,

My hand;

I'll sit up straight,

And then I'll stand!

I'll touch my ears,

My nose,

My chin,

Then quietly sit down again.

Left and Right

I put my right hand in,

I put my right hand out,

I give my hands a clap, clap, clap,

Then turn myself about.

I put my left hand in,

I put my left hand out,

I give my hands a clap, clap, clap,

Then turn myself about.

Listen, Listen

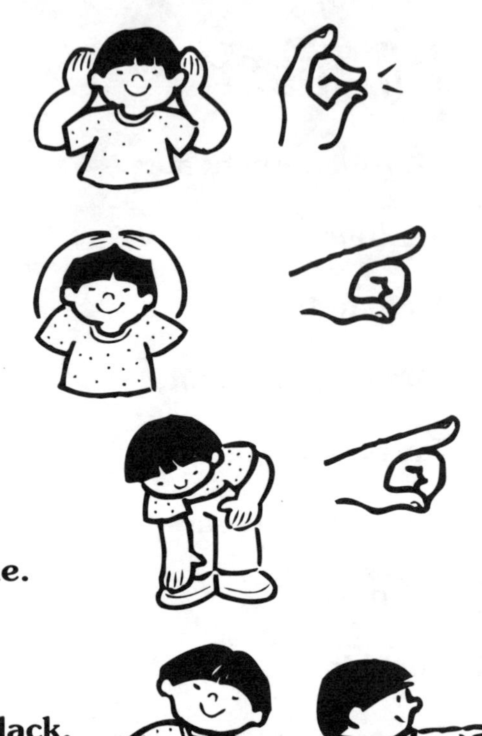

Listen, listen. We'll play a game.

When I snap my fingers, call out your name.

Listen, listen. Put your hands up on your head.

Now with one hand, point to something red.

Listen, listen. Put one hand on your shoe.

Now with the other hand, point to something blue.

Listen, listen. Put your hands behind your back.

Now with both your hands, point to something black.

My Hands

My hands upon my head I place,

On my shoulders, on my face,

On my knees and at my side,

Then behind me they will hide.

Then I raise them up so high

And let my fingers fly, fly, fly;

Then I'll clap them one, two, three,

See how quiet they can be!

One, Two, Three

Clap your hands; count one, two, three;

Pull your ear and slap your knee.

Stamp your feet, one, two, three, four;

Wiggle your fingers and touch the floor.

Raise your hands up to the skies,

Touch your nose, then touch your eyes.

Stamp your feet, one, two, three, four;

Wiggle your fingers and touch the floor.

Elbows out, just like a bird,

Touch your mouth without a word.

Softly clap and stamp your feet,

Tiptoe quietly, then take a seat.

Rag Doll

I'm a floppy, floppy rag doll
Dropping in my chair;
My head just rolls
From side to side—
My arms fall through the air.

Relax

Close your eyes, head drops down.

Face is smooth, not a frown.

Roll to left, your head's a ball!

Roll to right, sit up tall.

Lift your chin, look and see.

Deep, deep breath, one, two, three.

Big, big smile; hands in lap.

Make believe you've had a nap.

Now you've rested from your play—

Time to work again today!

Sleepy

I'm sleepy, very sleepy;

I want to stretch and yawn.

I'll close my eyes and just pretend

That daylight time has gone.

I'll breathe so softly, be so still,

A little mouse might creep

Across the floor, because he thought

That I was fast asleep.

This Is the Circle

This is the circle that is my head,

This is my mouth where words are said.

These are my eyes with which I see,

This is my nose that's part of me.

This is my hair that grows on my head,

This is my coat, all pretty and red.

This is the zipper I zip this way,

Now I'm all ready to go out and play.

Touch Your Nose

Touch your nose, touch your chin,

That's the way this game begins.

Touch your eyes and touch your knees,

Now pretend you're going to sneeze.

Touch your hair, touch one ear,

Touch your smiling lips right here,

Touch your elbows where they bend,

That's the way this touch game ends.

Use Your Eyes

Use your eyes, use your eyes,
You can look and see.
If you have on brown shoes,
Come and stand by me.
Use your ears, use your ears,
Listen now and hear!
What kind of a sound
Do you think you hear?
Use your nose, use your nose,
What is that you smell?
When you think that you know,
Raise your hand and tell.

When I Run and Jump and Play

When I run and jump and play,

I get thirsty everyday,
So I run to the kitchen sink,
Turn on the faucet and get a drink.
One glass, two glasses,

Three glasses, four,
And when I'm thirsty,
I'll drink some more.

God Gave Me Feet

God gave me feet that can turn me around;

God gave me hands that can touch the ground.

God gave me legs that can jump to the side;

God gave me knees that can bend and glide.

God gave me food and a place to live;

God gave me people with love to give.

So I thank God, 'cause it's easy to see

God is good and He cares about me!

God Made Bones

God made the bones in my fingers,

God made the bones in my toes.

When I touch my face,

I feel a bone in my nose!

God made the bones in a fish,

God made the bones in a pelican.

All my bones hooked together

Make my very own skeleton!

God Made My Ears

God made my ears, God made my nose.

God made my fingers, God made my toes.

God made my eyes, they're both open wide.

God made my mouth with white teeth inside.

God made my tongue that helps me to speak.

God made my chin, and God made my cheeks.

God made my hands that help me to play.

God made my feet for walking today.

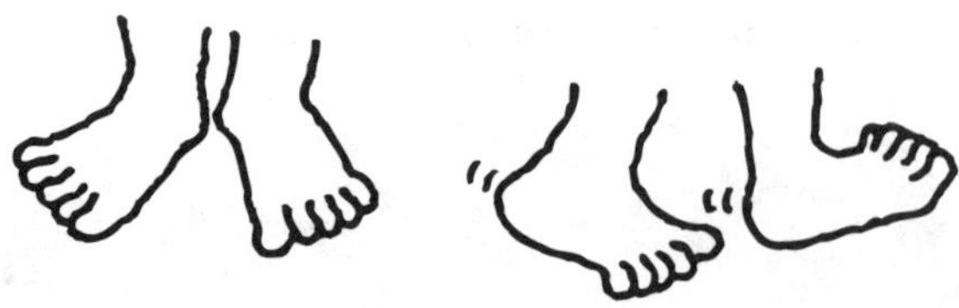

Growing

When I was one,

I was so small

I could not speak

A word at all.

When I was two,

I learned to talk;

I learned to sing;

I learned to walk.

When I was three,

I grew and grew;

I learned that Jesus

Loves me, too!

Now I am four;

I learn each day

Kind ways to help

And work and play.

Now I am big

Enough to say,

"Please come to church

With me today."

Here Is Our World

Here is our world, our great big world,

And here are the mountains high.

Here is a tree, a tall, tall tree,

And here is a bird that can fly.

There is the sun, the big bright sun,

That shines on the world all day.

Here are the children, running along,

God takes care of them as they play.

Sally, Sally

Sally, Sally, what can you do

With the feet God made for you?

I can skip and hop and run,

I can jump! It's lots of fun.

Sally, Sally, what can you do

With the arms God made for you?

I can catch a big round ball.

I can reach and stand up tall.

Can You?

Can you hop like a rabbit?

Can you jump like a frog?

Can you walk like a duck?

Can you run like a dog?

Can you stand straight and tall

Making no sound at all?

Shhhhhhh.

Five Little Ducks

Five little ducks went swimming one day,

Over the pond and far away.

Mother Duck said, "Quack, quack, quack, quack,"

But only four ducks came back.

Replace the underlined words with the following:

2. **Four little ducks/But only three**
3. **Three little ducks/But only two**
4. **Two little ducks/But only one**
5. **One little duck/But no little**
6. **No little ducks/But no little**
7. **Five little ducks/Because her five**

Five Little Sheep

Five little sheep drink on the river's shore,

One jumped across and then there were four.

Four little sheep jump beneath a tree,

One hid behind a rock and then there were three.

Three little sheep skip beneath a sky so blue,

One skipped away and then there were two.

Two little sheep running in the sun,

One went to take a nap and then there was one.

One little sheep wasn't having any fun,

He walked off to find his mama and then there were none.

Five Little Snowmen

Five little snowmen knocking at the door,

One melts away and then there are four.

Four little snowmen climbing up a tree,

One melts away and then there are three.

Three little snowmen out looking for you,

One melts away and then there are two.

Two little snowmen jumping in the sun,

One melts away and then there is one.

One little snowman standing all alone,

He melts away and then there are none.

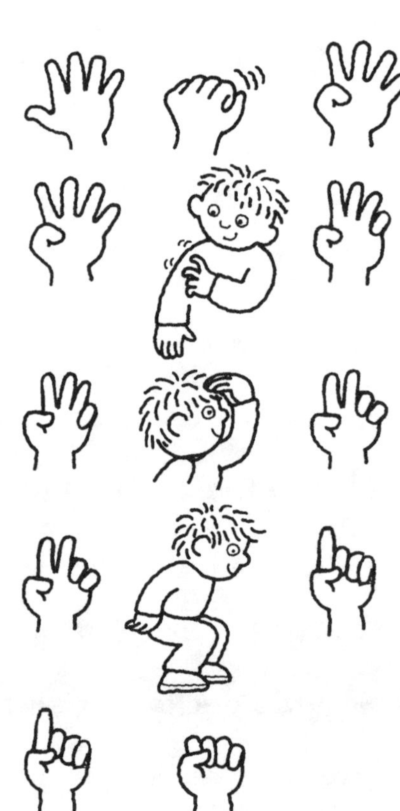

The Good Shepherd

One wooly sheep went hopping

And skipping,

Away from the shepherd and sheep.

And then he fell down and was

Lost in the night,

While the others went home to sleep.

The shepherd went out and looked

For his sheep—

He climbed up and down over boulders.

He found that tired sheep and

Lifted him up—

Then carried him home on his shoulders.

I'm a Camel

I'm a camel, big and humpy. 

I'm an elephant, walking clumpy. 

I'm a turtle, round and slow. 

God made us that way, you know. 

I'm a squeaky mouse so small. 

I'm a horse that's standing tall. 

I'm a bird—I flap my wings. 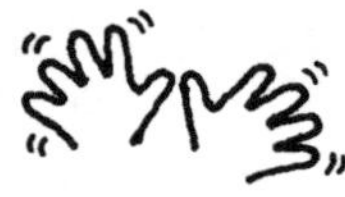

Thank You, God, who made all things. 

Trees

Elm trees stretch
And stretch so wide,
Their limbs reach out
On every side.

Pine trees stretch
And stretch so high,
They nearly reach up
To the sky.

Willows droop
And droop so low,
Their branches sweep
The ground below.

Twinkling Stars

Our God has made the twinkling stars.
He made the moon so bright
To tell us it is sleepy time
When we can rest each night.

Our God has made the day and night
To show His love and care;
So when I play and when I sleep,
I know that God is there.

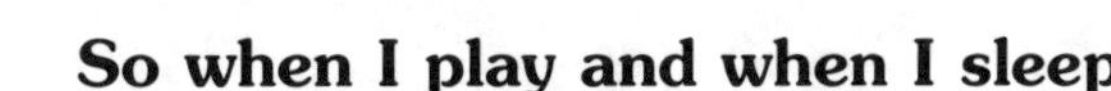

Eastertime

Easter is a time of joy

For all people, girls and boys.

Joyfully today we sing,

Jesus is our risen King!

Jesus is living!

Yes, He is living!

Jesus is living!

The Bible tells me so.

May be sung to "Jesus Loves Me" tune.

Happy Parade

Here is the donkey

Clip-clopping along.

The children are skipping

And singing a song.

Here are the branches;

Oh, see how they sway!

Here rides the Lord Jesus

On this happy day.

Ring the Bells

Ring, ring, ring the bells,

Ring them loud and clear

To tell the people everywhere

That Christmastime is here.

Clap, clap, clap your hands,

Clap them loud and clear

To tell the people everywhere

That Christmastime is here.

Stamp, stamp, stamp your feet,

Stamp them loud and clear

To tell the people everywhere

That Christmastime is here.

That First Christmas

Here is kind Joseph,

And here is sweet Mary;

She rode and he walked

On their Bethlehem journey.

Here is the inn.

Joseph knocked on the door.

But each bed was full;

There was no room for more.

They were both tired;

It was late in the day.

So they went to the stable

To sleep on the hay.

And there in the stable

That first Christmas morn,

Jesus, our Savior,

God's own Son was born.

'Tis Christmas

'Tis Christmas! 'Tis Christmas!

The candles all glow—

The birthday of Jesus,

Let everyone know!

'Tis Christmas! 'Tis Christmas!

Our Bible recalls

The birthday of Jesus,

God's love gift to all.

What Am I Baking?

Sift the flour and

Break an egg.

Add some salt and

Bit of nutmeg.

A spoon of butter,

A cup of milk—

Stir and beat as

Fine as silk.

Want to know what I'm

Going to bake?

Sh-sh, it's a secret!

A birthday cake!

Get-Acquainted Activities

What is the most welcome sound to a child's ears? His or her name! Get-acquainted activities provide opportunities for children to respond to their names and to learn the names of others in the group. These experiences help each child to feel that he or she belongs—that *this* is a place where he or she is loved, valued and accepted.

Circle of Friends

Procedure: Children sit in a circle. **We're going to play a game to help us remember the names of our friends.**

Call out one name. Named child skips around the circle and then returns to his or her place in the circle. **God loves** (name child). Repeat game, naming a different child for each round.

Variation: Call out a name and a way to move (tiptoe, baby steps, giant steps, etc.). Named child moves around the circle in the manner called.

Clap Your Name

Procedure: Begin by saying the name of a child and clapping for each syllable in the name as you say it. Children repeat after you, saying the name with the appropriate number of claps. As group becomes familiar with the procedure, use a child's first and last names.

Variation: Clap the syllables for the names of the seasons, months of the year, days of the week or familiar foods which have several syllables (macaroni, peanut butter, etc.).

Friend Find

Procedure: To help children welcome each other, lead children in doing the motions and singing these words to the tune of "Where Is Thumbkin?"

Where is Lisa? Where is Lisa? *(Shade eyes with one hand and look around the circle.)*

Here she is. Here she is. *(Point to Lisa.)*

We are glad to see you. *(Hold hands to make circle around eyes like glasses.)*

We are glad to see you.

Hello to you! Hello to you! *(Wave to Lisa.)*

Continue around the circle, singing song to welcome each child.

For Older Children: Child who is being sung to sings second line as a response: **Here I am. Here I am.**

The Friend Song

Procedure: Lead children in singing these words to the tune of "The Addams Family" theme song, inserting the names of children in the group:

These are my friends. *(clap, clap)*
These are my friends. *(clap, clap)*
These are my friends.
These are my friends.
These are my friends. *(clap, clap)*

There's Abby and there's David,
There's Juan and there's Julie,
There's Hannah and there's Ashley,
And then there's Jennifer.

These are my friends. *(clap, clap)*
These are my friends. *(clap, clap)*
These are my friends.
These are my friends.
These are my friends. *(clap, clap)*

Hot Potato

Materials: Children's music cassette/CD and player, beanbag or tennis ball.

Procedure: Children sit in a circle. Play music. Children pass beanbag or ball around the circle. After beanbag or ball has been passed to several children, stop the music. Child holding the beanbag or ball when the music stops tells his or her name and a favorite thing to do.

Variation: Child names a favorite color, food or animal.

Name Chant

Materials: Beanbag.

Procedure: Lead children in repeating this rhyme:

We'll go round in a circle,
Round in a game;
When we come to you,
Please say your name.

Give the beanbag to one child who says his or her name and then passes the beanbag to the child next to him or her. Next child says his or her name and then passes beanbag on until the beanbag has been passed all the way around the circle and every child has had an opportunity to say his or her name.

For Older Children: Challenge older children who are familiar with each other's names to say "Sitting next to me is Lauren," introducing his or her neighbor instead of telling his or her own name. The group repeats the name in unison: "Lauren!" Then child passes beanbag to the child he or she has just introduced and introductions continue until everyone has been introduced.

Name Cheer

Procedure: Lead children in this cheer:

Stand up! *(clap, clap)*
Be proud! *(clap, clap)*
Say your name *(clap, clap)*
Out loud! *(clap, clap)*

Invite a child to stand up and say his or her name after the cheer.

My name is Kelly! *(clap, clap)*

Repeat the cheer until each child has had a turn to say his or her name.

Nimble Names

Materials: Unbreakable candlestick with a short unlit candle in it.

Procedure: Place candlestick on the floor. Children sit in a large circle around the candlestick, leaving empty at least 4 feet (1.2 m) on each side of the candlestick. Select one volunteer by saying,

Mason, be nimble,
Mason, be quick,
Mason, jump over
The candlestick.

At this invitation, Mason gets up, runs and jumps over the candlestick and then sits down. Repeat with other children, calling out child's name to signal each child's turn. Continue until all children have had a turn.

For Older Children: After a child takes his or her turn, that child chooses the next child to take a turn, saying the rhyme to him or her.

Partners

Procedure: Invite children to choose partners. If group number is uneven, you become a partner. Give directions as you model each movement with your partner.

1. **Partners, stand next to each other.**
2. **Partners, stand back-to-back.**
3. **Partners, sit next to each other.**
4. **Partners, sit on the floor facing each other with your legs straight out and your feet touching.**
5. **Partners, lock elbows.**

Pick a Name

Materials: Index cards or large strips of paper, marker, paper bag.

Preparation: Print each child's name on a separate index card or paper strip. Place index cards or paper strips in paper bag.

Procedure: Children sit in a circle on the floor or around a table. Remove one name card or strip from bag. Show paper to children. Children guess or read whose name they see. You may need to give hints. **This person's name starts with a *T*.** Hand paper to the child whose name is on it. Repeat until all children's names have been read.

For Older Children: Children may print their own names on index cards or paper strips.

Rainbow Wear

Procedure: What colors are in the rainbow? Children respond. **We look like a rainbow with all the colors we are wearing!**

As you call out each color of the rainbow in order (red, orange, yellow, green, blue, purple), guide children to line up in an arc shape according to the dominant color in their clothing. After rainbow is formed, children say the names of those standing on either side of them.

For Older Children: Children remember which children they were standing next to in the rainbow. Children randomly move around the room and then quickly get back into original places when you call, **Rainbow order!**

Rocks Can't Talk

Materials: One small rock, puppet, block or other colorful object for each child.

Procedure: Give each child one object.

Since rocks can't talk, we're going to talk for them! Christopher, tell me something about your rock. Continue until each child has had a turn to be identified by name and tell something about his or her object to the group. If a child has difficulty, ask questions to help a child tell color, shape, texture, weight, etc.

For Older Children: After a child has had a turn, child names the next child in the group to have a turn.

Say Your Name

Procedure: Look at each child in turn and say,

Zippidy, zappedy, zoppedy, zee,
Will you say your name with me?

After child says his or her name with you, repeat rhyme to each child until all have had a turn.

For Older Children: Invite children to change the first letter of each word in the first line in the rhyme. Give an example. **Lippidy, lappedy, loppedy, lee.**

Talk Show

Materials: Marker, cardboard tube or other prop for a pretend microphone.

Procedure: Announce that you are the host of a TV show. Give the show a silly name and pick a topic (food, pets, toys, etc.). Ask general information questions and put the "microphone" in front of the child who wants to answer. **Today let's talk about foods that are green. Christopher, what green food do you like to eat?** Continue until all children have had a chance to be interviewed.

Tell a Story

Procedure: Tell either a true or a fictional short story about a pet. As you tell the story, act out keywords instead of saying them. Children try to identify the missing words. **My dog (walked) on the grass. When he saw a bird, he (ran) down the hill. Later, he (crawled) under the fence.** As you tell the story, use as many action words (skip, jump, hop, leap, slide, tiptoe, etc.) as you can.

Variation: Lead children to pantomime the action words with you.

Toy Basket

Materials: Basket or box, toys or books.

Procedure: Place basket or box on the floor. Each child chooses one toy or book from the room and puts it in the container. Children sit in a circle around the container.

One at a time, hold up each object. Child who put that object in the container raises his or her hand. Comment positively on each child's contribution. **I've seen Lily work our puzzles. She does a good job. She really knows about working puzzles.**

Wear Pairs

Procedure: Children sit in a circle. Call attention to one child. **Jenny, you have green buttons on your dress. Can you find another person wearing something green?** Jenny looks around the circle for a child wearing something green and then moves to sit by him or her.

Comment on another child's clothing color or comment on features such as zippers, pockets, patterns, etc. Child finds another child wearing something similar and sits by that child. Continue until all children have a partner. (If there is an uneven number of children or if someone cannot find a match, find a way to match with yourself.)

When all children have partners, children take turns telling their partner's name to the group.

For Younger Children: Help form pairs by calling attention to two children who are wearing something similar. Those two children move to sit together and become partners.

We'll Clap for You!

Materials: Beanbag or other small soft object.

Procedure: Lead children in saying the following rhyme:

Hello, good friends,
And how are you?
Say your name,
And we'll clap for you.

Toss the beanbag to a child. Child says his or her name and then the group claps. Child tosses beanbag to another child. Repeat the rhyme; child holding beanbag says name and group claps. Continue game until all have had a turn to say their name.

Western Welcome

Materials: Children's music cassette/CD and player, cowboy hat.

Procedure: Lead children in a game similar to Hot Potato. Children sit cross-legged in a circle and pass the cowboy hat around the circle while the music plays.

When you stop the music, the child with the hat says "Hi, my name is Tyler." The rest of the group waves to Tyler and replies "Howdy, Tyler." Tyler stretches out his legs to show he has had a turn. Repeat activity until everyone has had a turn.

Who's Your Friend?

Procedure: Julia, who's your friend? Child you've named chooses another child in the group. Ask the two children to stand by each other. **I see that both Julia and Morgan have blue eyes. Julia and Morgan are friends.** Repeat by calling on another child. After named child chooses a partner, comment on their similarities. Continue until all children have been paired.

Variation: Instead of identifying similarities, tell what is different about the two children. **I see that Julia has brown hair and Morgan has blond hair. Julia and Morgan are friends.**

For Older Children: Children in the group tell what is the same or different between the two friends.

Movement Activities

Young children are physically active and need plenty of opportunities for movement of their whole bodies. Movement activities require open space, indoors or outdoors, so children can enjoy expending their energy as they develop large motor skills.

Animal Actions

Procedure: Children walk slowly in a circle. Call out the name of an animal. Children think of and perform motions like that animal. **Monkey.** Children act like they are swinging from trees, eating bananas, climbing up trees, etc. Repeat with other animals (dogs, cats, fish, cows, rabbits, horses, etc.).

For Younger Children: Call out both the name of the animal and the way to move as you model the motions for children to imitate. Hop while calling, **Hop like bunnies.** Put your hands together and move them side to side in front of you while calling, **Swim like fish.** Crouch down on the floor as if you're going to jump while calling, **Jump like frogs.**

Blue and Yellow

Procedure: Seat children in a circle. Divide circle in half. Tell children on the left side of the circle that they are the blue team. Tell children on the right side that they are the yellow team. **When I call the name of your team, stand up quickly.** Call out "blue" and "yellow" several times. After each call, children on the called team sit down. Then challenge children by calling out a color other than blue or yellow. Continue as time and interest allows.

Variation: Use names of animals for team names.

Body Moves

Materials: Large index cards, marker.

Preparation: On index cards, draw stick figures in different positions (crouching, lying down, doing jumping jacks, touching toes, hands over head, etc.), one figure per card.

Procedure: Stand in front of children. Hold up one of the cards. Children imitate the motion of the figure on the card. Continue the activity, showing the next card in the stack. After children have made all the moves on the cards, invite a volunteer to make a motion for the group to imitate. Continue as time and interest allows.

Body Parts

Procedure: Children stand in a large circle. **Touch your nose.** Children touch their noses. **Touch your hair.** Children touch their hair. Continue with a few simple actions and then move onto more complicated actions. **Touch your nose to your knee. Touch your knee to your elbow. Touch your ear to your shoulder. Touch your elbow to your heel.**

David's Sheep

Materials: Length of yarn.

Preparation: Use yarn to make a line at one side of an open area in your room.

Procedure: Children line up side by side along yarn line. Stand at other side of open area.

At your signal, children call to you, "David, David, how many sheep do you have?" Respond with a number under ten. **Five sheep.** Children jump forward five times. Children repeat their call to you and you respond with a different number each time.

After a few times, answer, **None! The lion has them!** When children hear that, they run back to the yarn line, trying to avoid being tagged by you. Tagged children stand by you and wait to tag other children the next time you answer "None!" Continue activity until there are few or no children left untagged.

Dogs and Cats

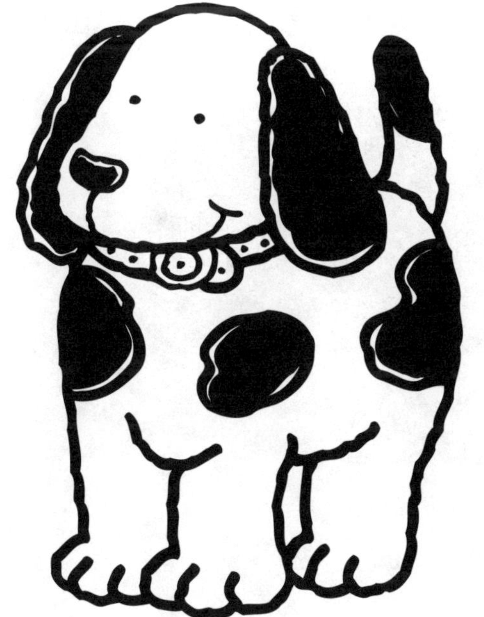

Procedure: I'm going to whisper the name of an animal to each person in our group. Remember the name of your animal. Whisper "dog" or "cat" to each child. **If your animal is a dog, make a sound like a dog.** Children respond**. If your animal is a cat, make a sound like a cat.** Children respond.

Gather children in a group. **Make the sound of your animal. Listen to find another person who is making the same sound. When you find someone making the same sound as you, hold hands and sit down.** Continue activity until all children are seated in pairs. (Join in the activity if needed to complete a pair.)

Food Fun

Procedure: With the children, practice doing the motions suggested by the words below.

1. **Sandwich** (*Stand back-to-back with a partner.*)
2. **Pretzel** (*Sit cross-legged on the floor.*)
3. **Pancake** (*Lie flat on back.*)
4. **Popcorn** (*Jump up and down in place.*)
5. **Grapes** (*Huddle in groups.*)

Invite children to walk around the playing area. Call out one of the above foods. Children respond with the appropriate motion. After a few seconds, call out another food. Children respond with that motion. Continue as time and interest allow.

Freeze

Materials: Paper napkins or tissues.

Procedure: We're going to find out if we can walk with a napkin on our heads without dropping it. Place a napkin or tissue on each child's head. Children walk across the room to become familiar with the idea. **If your napkin falls off your head, pretend you are frozen. You must stand still! You cannot move until I put your napkin back on your head.** Replace fallen napkin for frozen children. As activity progresses, invite children to unfreeze anyone who is frozen.

Hinges

Procedure: Children stand in a semicircle. Touch a hinge in the room and demonstrate its use. **Look around our room and see if you can find any other hinges.** When a child locates a hinge, he or she touches it and demonstrates its use. For example, he or she may open and close a door.

All of us are put together with hinges. Bend your elbow. Your elbow is a hinge. Bend your knee. Your knee is a hinge. Children name and bend other hinges in the body (wrist, shoulder, finger joints, etc.).

Then repeat the following rhyme, bending body hinge when named. All clap on the word "crack."

I'm all made of hinges and everything bends,
From the top of my head, way down to the ends.
I'm hinges in front and I'm hinges in back—
If I didn't have hinges, I surely would CRACK!

How Do You Look?

Procedure: Children stand with space between them. Choose a volunteer and ask, **How do you look when you are climbing a mountain?** Volunteer acts out that motion. **Now let's all climb a mountain.** All children do motion.

Repeat with new volunteer and other motions (digging a hole, brushing your hair, swimming in a lake, jumping rope, going to sleep, etc.).

For Younger Children: Lead children in singing the following words and making the climbing motion to the tune of "Here We Go 'Round the Mulberry Bush":

This is the way we climb a mountain,
Climb a mountain, climb a mountain.
This is the way we climb a mountain,
Early in the morning.

For Older Children: Ask a volunteer to think of a motion to say and do. Group imitates the volunteer and guesses what the motion represents.

How Would You Move?

Procedure: Children stand with space between them. **How would you move if you were a butterfly flying through the sunshine?** Children answer by moving around the room in that way.

Repeat question, substituting different animals or items (a frog eating a fly, a snake in the grass, a dripping ice cream cone, a raindrop in a rainstorm, a lost puppy, a flower in a garden, a fish in a river, etc.).

Hula Hoop Pass

Materials: Hula hoop.

Procedure: Children stand in a circle. **We're going to pass this hula hoop around the circle. We'll each take a turn stepping through it!** Demonstrate how to hold the hula hoop out in front of yourself with one hand and then step through it with one leg and then the other.

Give one child the hula hoop. Child steps through the hula hoop and hands it to the child next to him or her. Children continue taking turns around the circle.

Demonstrate holding hula hoop above your head, bringing it down over your body and then stepping out of it. Children repeat your action, taking turns around the circle.

For Younger Children: Ask two children to hold the hula hoop so that the other children can take turns stepping through it. Repeat the activity to give other children a turn to hold the hula hoop. Then place hula hoop on the ground and have children take turns jumping with two feet into and out of the hula hoop.

Jumpers in the Dell

Procedure: Children stand an arm's distance apart in a large area. Lead children in singing the following words to the tune of "The Farmer in the Dell" and using the actions the words suggest:

We're jumping up and down.
We're jumping up and down.
We smile because we're having fun.
We're jumping up and down.

Repeat the tune and substitute the following phrases for "We're jumping up and down":

1. **We bend and touch our toes.**
2. **We kick our legs up high.**
3. **We jog around the room.**
4. **We stretch up to the sky.**

Jumping High

Materials: Carpet squares, towels or masking tape and colored construction paper.

Preparation: Place carpet squares or towels in a line to form a continuous path, or tape construction paper down to form a path. (Note: Do not use towels on linoleum floors.)

Procedure: Children jump from one square or towel to the next. **Jump on the path using both feet.** When all children have jumped down the path, repeat activity, suggesting other motions (walking, hopping, walking backward or sideways, etc.) to be used to go down the path.

Look at It!

Procedure: Gather children in the center of your room. **Listen and do what I say as quickly as you can!** Direct attention to objects and people in the room by saying, **Look at the cubbies!** Children turn to look at the cubbies. Pause briefly before giving a new direction. **Look at the windows! Look at the light switch! Look at the blocks! Look at Kelly!** Continue naming objects and people in your room.

For Older Children: Children take turns naming objects and people to look at.

Reach High

Procedure: Can you reach high? Lead children in stretching arms above head. Continue activity with other movements, pausing briefly between each suggestion. **Can you turn around? Put your head between your knees? Stand up? Scratch your knee? Wiggle your shoulders? Touch your toes? Hide your eyes? Touch your elbow?**

For Older Children: Challenge children to close their eyes as they follow your directions.

Sidewalk Stand

Materials: Chalk.

Preparation: On sidewalk or blacktop, draw a row of squares, one for each child. Draw the squares large enough for a child to stand inside.

Procedure: Children stand around squares**. If your birthday is in January or February, come and stand in a square.** Children born in those months move to a square. Continue calling months until each child is standing in a square.

Stop and Go!

Materials: Red and green construction paper, marker, scissors.

Preparation: Use red and green construction paper to make a Stop sign and a Go sign. Clear the room or playing area of furniture.

Procedure: Children line up side by side on one side of the room or playing area. Stand on the opposite side of the room or playing area. **When I hold up this Go sign, everyone may walk toward me. But when I hold up the Stop sign, everyone must freeze in place.**

Begin the activity by holding up the Go sign, allowing children to walk toward you. Hold up the Stop sign for children to freeze in place. If children do not freeze when you hold up the Stop sign, gently remind them that the Stop sign is up. Do not make children start over. Continue activity until children reach you. Play again as time and interest allow.

Variation: The first child to reach you may be the sign holder for the next round.

For Younger Children: Call out "Stop" and "Go" as well as holding up the signs.

For Older Children: Challenge the children. **I am going to hold up one sign but say the opposite action. Your job is to obey the sign! Try not to get confused by my words.** Hold up one sign and say the opposite action. Sometimes say the same action as the sign indicates to keep the challenge high.

Tape Travel

Materials: Masking tape, measuring stick.

Preparation: Place 10-foot (3-m) lengths of tape on the ground in parallel lines about 5 feet (1.5 m) apart from each other. Make one length for every five children.

Procedure: Children line up single file so that five children are at one end of each masking-tape length. At your signal, the first child in each line walks with his or her feet on the tape. Children continue taking turns until each child in the line has had a turn.

Play again by lining up all children at one end of the last tape length. First child begins walking along the tape length with his or her feet on the tape. When that child gets to the end of one tape length, he or she begins the next tape length, walking back in the opposite direction so that children are snaking along the tape lengths.

What Am I?

Procedure: Guide two volunteers to lie on the floor in the shape of a *T*. Ask other children to guess the letter they have formed. Repeat with other volunteers and other easy-to-form letters, such as *I*, *C* and *Y*.

Children then work in pairs or trios to decide on a letter and then form it. When they've completed their letter, other children guess it.

Variation: Children form numbers and shapes.

What's the Weather?

Procedure: Children stand at least an arm's length apart. **I am the Weatherperson.** Children ask you, "What's the weather?" Respond with one of the following answers and lead children in doing actions words suggest.

1. **Windy!** (*Children make wind noises.*)
2. **Thunderstorm!** (*Children clap their hands and stomp their feet.*)
3. **Hot and sunny!** (*Children fan them selves.*)
4. **Hurricane!** (*Children twirl around in place several times and then sit down.*)

Repeat play with a child volunteer as the Weatherperson. Continue as time and interest allow, choosing a new Weatherperson for each round.

For Younger Children: Demonstrate and practice with the children each of the weather conditions and actions before playing the game.

What's Your Answer?

Procedure: Children stand or sit in a circle. **Are you wearing something green today?** If a child answers yes to your question, he or she finds a new place to sit. Repeat with other questions. **Do you have a brother? Are you the oldest child in your family? Do you have a baby in your family? Are you wearing jeans today?** Be sure every child has an opportunity to move.

Children will also enjoy personalized questions. **Do you have a brother named Jon? Do you have a pet goat?**

Where Is It?

Materials: Construction paper in a variety of colors.

Procedure: Show a piece of red construction paper to children. **What color is this? Your job is to find something red in our room. When you find something red, touch it and keep touching it.** Children respond to your directions. **While you're touching something red, you can help another person touch something red by holding that person's hand. You can make a chain by holding hands with the people who need to touch something red.**

When all children have found something red by touching it either directly or as part of a chain, repeat the activity by showing another color.

Which Way?

Materials: Large sheet of paper, marker.

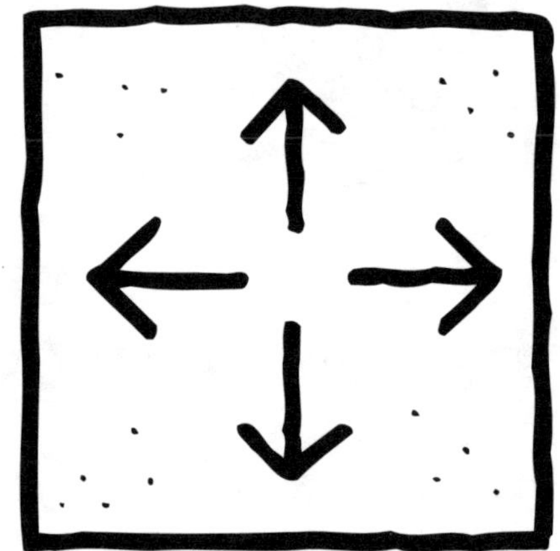

Preparation: Draw four arrows as shown in sketch.

Procedure: Children stand at least an arm's length apart. Be sure all children can easily see the arrows on the paper. As you point to an arrow, children move both their arms in that direction.

For Younger Children: Before moving on to the next arrow, pause in order to give all children the opportunity to catch up.

For Older Children: Challenge children to say the directions (up, down, left, right) with you.

Music Activities

Music and rhythm activities help regain wandering attention faster than almost anything else! Young children are attracted to music and movement, even if they don't always sing along. Using music activities can also boost the group's joy factor by leaps and bounds!

Animal Walk

Procedure: Children stand in an open area. Ask volunteers to show how an elephant walks. **Let's all walk like an elephant.** Lead children in singing these words to the tune of "Here We Go 'Round the Mulberry Bush" and walking like an elephant.

This is the way the elephant walks,
The elephant walks, the elephant walks.
This is the way the elephant walks,
Walking at the zoo.

Ask volunteers to demonstrate how the following animals move: kangaroos, horses, rabbits. Then sing the song as all children move like the animal you're singing about.

For Older Children: Invite volunteers to name other animals and show how each moves. Group imitates those actions.

Beanbag Fun

Materials: Children's cassette/CD and player, a beanbag for each child.

Procedure: Gather children in an open area. Give each child a beanbag to place on his or her head. When the music begins, children move about the room in time to the music, trying to keep the beanbag on their heads. After the music stops, children place their beanbag in a different place (elbow, shoulder, top of foot or back). Begin the music as children repeat the activity.

Bend Your Knees

Procedure: Lead children in singing these words to the tune of "Here We Go 'Round the Mulberry Bush," using actions words suggest.

Bend your knees and clap your hands.
Bend your knees and clap your hands.
Turn around and touch your nose,
Touch your ears and touch your toes.

Bend your knees and clap your hands.
Bend your knees and clap your hands.
Reach up high and turn around,
Touch your elbows, touch the ground.

Bible Verse Rhythms

Procedure: Bible verses may often be quoted rhythmically. As you guide children in saying the following Bible verses, emphasize the capitalized words and syllables.

Be KIND to each OTH-er. (See Ephesians 4:32.)

Give THANKS to the LORD, for HE is GOOD. (Psalm 136:1)

Do GOOD to EV-'ry-ONE. (See Galatians 6:10.)

JE-sus IS the SON of GOD. (See John 1:34.)

Variation: Children clap, snap fingers, pat thighs or tap shoulders as you say the verses, emphasizing the capitalized words and syllables.

Catch the Rhythm!

Procedure: Children sit with you in a semicircle in front of you. Clap a simple rhythmic pattern (for example, long-short-long-short-long-short). Children imitate your rhythmic clapping. Repeat the pattern with children echoing; then increase the rhythm's complexity and encourage children to echo. Repeat with a new pattern.

For Older Children: Invite a child to clap out a rhythm for the syllables in his or first and last name. All children clap the rhythm as they say that child's name. Continue so that all children get a turn.

Children Wearing Red

Procedure: Look at the color of the clothes you are wearing today. Let volunteers name colors. **Listen to this song for a color you're wearing. Then do what our song says.** Sing these words to the tune of "The Farmer in the Dell":

Children wearing red stand up.
Children wearing blue stand up.
Children wearing green stand up,
So we can see your colors.

Children wearing blue sit down.
Children wearing green sit down.
Children wearing red sit down,
For we have seen your colors.

Adjust the words to include other colors children are wearing. Occasionally include the name of a color no one is wearing.

Echo Game

Procedure: Sit with children in a circle on the floor or in chairs. Pat your legs in a slow rhythm. Children imitate your actions. Begin speaking rhythmically, accenting the words and syllables in capital letters. Use your name.

MY name is MRS. Tate.

Children echo words with the same rhythm.

MRS. Tate, MRS. Tate.

Child sitting next to you says his or her name in the same rhythm.

MY name is ER-ic.

You and children echo words with the same rhythm.

ER-ic, ER-ic.

Continue around the circle until each child has had a turn. Vary the activity by clapping instead of patting your leg.

God Made My Hands

Procedure: Lead children in singing the words to the tune of "Did You Ever See a Lassie?" using actions words suggest.

God made my hands for clapping,
for clapping, for clapping.
God made my hands for clapping.
Hear how they clap! *(Clap.)*

God made my feet for tapping,
for tapping, for tapping.
God made my feet for tapping.
Hear how they tap! *(Tap feet.)*

God made my arms for swinging,
for swinging, for swinging.
God made my arms for swinging.
Watch while I swing. *(Swing arms.)*

Hidden Sounds

Materials: Ticking clock, music box or audiocassette and player.

Procedure: Hide the sound-making object somewhere in your room, preferably hiding the object while children are occupied with another activity. Turn it on or ask a helper to do so.

Quiet children and ask them to listen for the sound. Children hunt around the room for its source. Once object has been found, children may take turns hiding it for other children to locate.

How Does It Sound?

Procedure: Lead children to say, **Hello, God loves you.** Then invite children to repeat the sentence with the following movements. Ask children to listen to differences in the sounds they hear.

1. **Cup your hands behind your ears.**
2. **Place your hands in front of your ears, straight out from head.**
3. **Stand by a wall, cup your hands around your mouth and against the wall.**
4. **Step back from the wall and keep your hands around your mouth.**
5. **Cover your ears with your hands.**

I Look at the Ceiling

Procedure: Lead children in singing these words to the tune of "Here We Go 'Round the Mulberry Bush," using the actions words suggest.

I look at the ceiling, I look at the door.
I look at the windows, I look at the floor.
I look at my friends and I count one, two, three.
I'm glad God has made them; I'm glad God made me.

Here are my shoulders and here is my nose.
Here are my elbows and here are my toes.
Here are my friends and I count one, two, three.
I'm glad God has made them; I'm glad God made me.

I Wish I Were

Procedure: Ask a volunteer to demonstrate how a rabbit moves. Then lead children in singing the following words to the tune of "Did You Ever See a Lassie?" Use actions words indicate.

I wish I were a rabbit, a rabbit, a rabbit.
I wish I were a rabbit, I know what I'd do.

I'd hop and I'd hop and I'd hop and I'd hop.
I wish I were a rabbit and that's what I'd do.

Repeat song, inserting other animals and movements (frog/jump, bird/fly, fish/swim, horse/gallop).

Variation: Show pictures of a rabbit, frog, bird, fish and horse before singing about each animal.

Let Everyone Clap Hands

Procedure: Lead children in singing these words to the tune of "If You're Happy and You Know It."

Let everyone clap hands just like me. *(clap, clap)*
Let everyone clap hands just like me. *(clap, clap)*
Come on and join the game.
You'll find it's just the same.
Let everyone clap hands just like me. *(clap, clap)*

Repeat, substituting the following phrases and corresponding actions:

1. **Let everyone sneeze just like me.** *(ah-choo)*
2. **Let everyone laugh just like me.** *(ha-ha)*
3. **Let everyone cry just like me.** *(boo-hoo)*
4. **Let everyone stand up and jump.** *(jump, jump).*

Listening Ears

Procedure: Lead children in singing these words to the tune of "The Farmer in the Dell." After singing the last line of the song, call out a child's name. Child stands up and claps.

Put on your list'ning ears.
Put on your thinking cap.
When you hear me call your name,
Stand up and give a clap.

Repeat, calling a different child each time. After children are familiar with the song, vary the directions for the action in the last line.

1. **Give your foot a tap.**
2. **Give your foot a stamp.**
3. **Stand up and do a jump.**

Marching, Marching

Materials: Several small drums.

Procedure: Children form a line. Give drums to volunteers. Lead all children in marching and singing these words to the tune of "Twinkle, Twinkle, Little Star":

Marching, marching, here we come,
Marching, marching, hear our drum.
Marching, marching in a row,
Marching, marching, drumming as we go.

Left foot, right foot, marching feet,
Left foot, right foot, marching down the street.
Marching, marching, heads held high,
Marching, marching, watch as we go by.

Invite drummers to share their drums with other children as you repeat the song.

For Older Children: Challenge children to identify their left and right feet before they march.

Measuring Song

Procedure: Let's pretend we are measuring ourselves. Demonstrate using your hands to measure your head. Sing these words to the tune of "Here We Go 'Round the Mulberry Bush," using actions words suggest.

We measure our hand and we measure our nose.
We measure our feet and we measure our toes.
We measure our head and our ears and our chin,
And now let's all smile and we'll measure our grin.

Variation: Before using hands to measure, show a measuring tape, yardstick or ruler and demonstrate the use of the measuring tool.

Movement Rhythms

Procedure: Lead children in doing the motions and varying the tempo as words suggest.

Clap your hands s-l-o-w-l-y, s-l-o-w-l-y, s-l-o-w-l-y;
Then clap them very quickly, just like me.

Repeat, substituting the following movements:

1. **Flap your arms**
2. **Stomp your feet**
3. **Pat your head**
4. **Blink your eyes**

Musical Circles

Materials: Four or five 8-foot (2.4-m) yarn lengths, children's music cassette/CD and player.

Preparation: Lay yarn in circles on the floor.

Procedure: Play the music. Children walk around the outside of circles as music plays. When music stops, children stand inside the circle closest to them. Start the music again and remove a circle. When music stops, children stand in remaining circles. Repeat the activity, removing a circle each round until children have all squeezed into the last circle.

Be sure no child is left out. Musical Circles is an excellent alternative to Musical Chairs. All children are winners in Musical Circles.

Variations: Play Musical Squares, substituting large squares of butcher paper for circles. Or use hula hoops instead of yarn circles for Musical Circles.

Popcorn Game

Materials: Popcorn kernels, popped corn, children's cassette/CD and player.

Procedure: Show popcorn kernels. **How can you make yourself small like a popcorn kernel?** Demonstrate how to crouch down and hug your knees. Children practice kernel position.

What would you do to show that the popcorn kernel has popped? Show popped corn. Then demonstrate how to pop up from kernel position to a position like an open jumping jack. Shout "Pop!" as you jump up. Children practice this.

Play music. Children crouch in the kernel position. Stop the music. When children hear the music stop, they shout "Pop!" as they pop up. Play music again for children to go immediately back to being popcorn kernels. Repeat as time and interest allow.

Put Your Hands

Procedure: Lead children in singing the following words to the tune of "Skip to My Lou" or "Here We Go 'Round the Mulberry Bush." Use actions words suggest.

Put your hands over your head.
Put your hands over your head.
Put your hands over your head.
Then clap two hands together.

Repeat, substituting the following phrases in each new verse:

1. **Put your hands on your knees.**
2. **Put your hands behind your back.**
3. **Put your hands on your hips.**
4. **Put your hands on your face.**

For Older Children: Children stand facing a partner to sing this final verse, singing their partner's name and clapping each other's hands.

I have a friend, her name is Anna.
I have a friend, her name is Anna.
I have a friend, her name is Anna.
We can clap together.

Rhythmic Passing

Materials: A drum, a small object (child's shoe, ball, beanbag, etc.).

Procedure: Children sit in a circle. Beat the drum in a slow steady rhythm. Lead the children in counting the beats aloud. **One, two, three, four; one, two, three, four,** etc. Give a child the small object. **When we say "four," you may pass the (shoe) to the person sitting next to you.** Continue drumming and counting beats until each child has had a turn to pass the object.

Roll, Roll, Roll Your Hands

Procedure: Lead children in singing the following words to the tune of "Row, Row, Row Your Boat." Use actions words suggest.

Roll, roll, roll your hands,
Slowly as can be.
Roll them, roll them, roll them, roll them,
Do it now with me.

Roll, roll, roll your hands,
Fast as fast can be.
Roll them, roll them, roll them, roll them,
Do it now with me.

Repeat, substituting the following words and motions:

1. **Clap, clap, clap your hands**
2. **Shake, shake, shake your hands**
3. **Stamp, stamp, stamp your feet**

Salad Bowl Singing

Materials: A disposable bowl or cup for each child.

Procedure: Lead children in singing a familiar song. Then children place bowls or cups in front of their faces. Repeat singing the song as each child sings into his or her bowl or cup. **How did your voice sound when you sang into your (bowl)?** Invite a few children to remove their bowls or cups and to listen to others as they repeat the song with their bowls or cups. **How did our song sound when people sang into their (bowls)? Which way of singing do you like best?**

Silly Sounds

Procedure: Lead children in singing a familiar song. **Now let's try singing a little differently.** Lead children in singing the song while they are pinching their noses closed. **How does that make our voices sound different?**

Repeat activity, leading children to sing while covering ears, standing on one foot, closing eyes or covering mouth. **Which way sounded the silliest? Which ways sounded the same? What way was hardest to hear our voices?**

Sometimes I'm Very Tall

Procedure: Lead children in singing the following words to the tune of "The Farmer in the Dell" and doing accompanying motions:

Sometimes I'm very tall. *(Stand up tall.)*
Sometimes I'm very small. *(Squat down.)*
Sometimes I'm tall, *(Stand up tall.)*
Sometimes I'm small, *(Squat down.)*
Guess what I am now. *(Child chooses to stand up or squat down.)*

Streamer Songs

Materials: Crepe-paper streamers, scissors, children's cassette/CD and player.

Preparation: Cut crepe-paper streamers into approximately 2-foot (.6-m) lengths, one for each child.

Procedure: Gather children in an open area. Give each child a streamer. Play music. Children move about the room, waving their streamers in time to the music.

This Is My Right Hand

Procedure: Review right and left with children. Lead children in singing the following words to the tune of "Here We Go 'Round the Mulberry Bush." Use actions words suggest.

This is my right hand, I'll raise it up high.
This is my left hand, I'll reach to the sky.
Right hand and left hand, I'll roll them around,
Right hand and left hand, I'll pound and I'll pound.

Two Little Hands

Procedure: Lead children in singing the following words to the tune of "Twinkle, Twinkle Little Star." Use actions words suggest.

Two little hands go clap, clap, clap,
Two little feet go tap, tap, tap.
Two little hands go thump, thump, thump,
Two little feet go jump, jump, jump.

Two little hands go clap, clap, clap,
Two little feet go tap, tap, tap.
One little body turns around,
One little person sits quietly down.

Windows

Procedure: Children stand in a circle, facing one direction. Guide two children to form a window by standing and facing each other. They raise their hands above their heads and lock fingers. Lead children in singing the following words to the tune of "In and Out the Window" as children step through the window and keep walking around in a circle.

I'm stepping through the window.

I'm stepping through the window.

I'm stepping through the window,

And I see my friend Joey.

Continue activity until all children have had a turn to step through the window and have their name said. If time and interest allow, choose two other children to form the window and repeat the activity.

Quiet Activities

Quiet activities provide children with a welcome change of pace when they need a break from active involvement. Children will enjoy quiet activities individually or in small groups.

Alphabet Artist

Materials: Paper, pencils.

Procedure: Ask a volunteer to tell one letter of the alphabet. Children draw a picture of something that begins with that letter. Give hints if a child has difficulty. **We are sitting at something that begins with *T*.** Repeat with another volunteer and letter.

Variation: Play the game with numbers instead of letters. Volunteer chooses a number between 1 and 10. Children draw one object (ball, square, etc.) that number of times.

Assorted Sorting

Materials: Small paper plates, various items to sort by color or shape (dry cereal, crayons, pasta, dried beans, etc.).

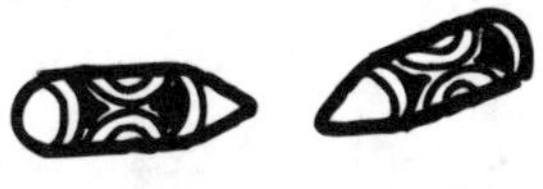

Procedure: Give each child several paper plates and a variety of items to sort. Child places matching items on the same paper plates.

Blow Ball

Materials: A straw for each child, cotton balls.

Procedure: Children sit around a table. Give each child a straw. Place a cotton ball in the center of the table. Children blow into straws in an attempt to move the cotton ball across the table. When children are familiar with the idea, each child has a turn to blow the cotton ball to another child. Be sure each child has a turn.

For Older Children: Place a wastebasket or large box on the floor at the edge of the table. Children take turns blowing the cotton ball the length of the table and into a wastepaper basket or box.

Can You Remember?

Procedure: I'm going to name three things you know how to do. Listen and do what I say. Turn around, clap your hands and sit down. Children respond. Repeat activity with other movements (stand up, stamp your feet, touch your toes, touch your elbow, etc.).

For Older Children: As children become adept at remembering and doing a three-item sequence, give four or five instructions at a time.

 Color Choice

Materials: Crayons the colors of the rainbow (red, orange, yellow, blue, purple), a paper bag, white paper.

Procedure: Place crayons in bag. Invite a child to take a crayon from the bag without looking into the bag. **Shauna, what color is your crayon? You picked a purple crayon! You can color purple all over your paper.** Child works to fill paper with purple color. Continue similarly, letting other children choose a crayon and fill paper with that color.

When work is complete, arrange papers in rainbow order.

For Older Children: Challenge child to create a pattern of shapes and designs to fill the paper with the chosen crayon color.

Eat It or Not

Procedure: I went to the store and bought a (broom). Do you think I should eat it? Why not? What do you think I should do with it? Repeat, using food and nonfood items, silly and serious.

For Older Children: Ask a volunteer to lead the group. Show pictures from a store catalog or advertisement to give ideas of items bought at a store.

Eyes Open, Eyes Closed

Materials: Four to six small objects, tray, towel.

Procedure: Place objects on tray in front of children. They look at objects for 30 seconds; then place a towel over the objects. Reach under towel to remove one object. Remove towel. Children look at objects and tell which one is missing. Repeat game.

Variation: Add an object instead of remove one.

Hidden Picture

Materials: Large calendar or magazine picture, sheet of paper the same size as the picture.

Procedure: Cover picture with the paper. Show children covered picture, slowly moving the paper to reveal a small part of the picture. Children tell what they see and take turns guessing what the picture could be.

Continue to slowly move paper away from the picture, so children can see more and more of the picture. Children continue to talk about what the picture might be. Repeat process until entire picture is revealed or children have guessed the picture contents.

Instant Puppets

Materials: Water-based, nontoxic marker.

Procedure: Use marker to draw a face on your finger for an instant puppet. Then draw a face on one finger of each child. Use your puppet to speak to children's puppets. **What are you playing today? What color is your shirt?**

Variation: Draw faces on adhesive dots or cut-off envelope corners. Children stick dot to finger or slip finger into envelope corner for an instant puppet.

Let's Tell a Story

Materials: A small object for each child (toy car, plastic animal or person, spoon, crayon, etc.), paper bag.

Preparation: Place all objects in the bag.

Procedure: Sit in a circle with the children. Take one object from the bag and begin to tell a story about the object. After a few sentences, pass the bag to the child next to you. Child picks a new object from the bag and names the object. Continue telling the story, including in the story the object the child just picked out of the bag. After a few more sentences, signal the child to pass the bag on. Continue until each child has had a turn to pick something from the bag and name it, and you have introduced it into the story.

Listen Up

Procedure: Children lay or sit on floor with eyes closed. Make sure there is space between children. **Let's listen to noises we can hear in this room. It's OK if we're quiet for a long time before we hear a sound. Raise your hand when you hear a sound.** Children report what sounds they hear. If few sounds are able to be heard in your room, open door or window.

Match Me

Procedure: Sydney, I see you are wearing a yellow sweater today. Find something in our room that is the same color as your sweater. Repeat with other colors on children's clothing.

Matchup

Materials: Construction paper strips in a variety of colors.

Procedure: Children sit in a semicircle around a table. Have more chairs at the table than children. Sit so that children can easily see you.

I'm going to show you two strips of paper. If the colors are the same, stay where you are. If the colors are different, get up and move to another chair. Show paper strips, two at a time, and allow children time to respond as needed. Continue game as time and interest allow.

Measure Up!

Materials: A ruler for each child; optional—cardboard, scissors, pencil.

Preparation: None. (Optional: If rulers are not available, make a cardboard ruler for each child by cutting cardboard into 1x12-inch [2.5x30.5-cm] strips.)

Procedure: Give each child a ruler. Ask children to find an object in the room that is as long as the ruler. Then ask children to find items that are longer or shorter than the ruler.

Variation: Give children paper and pencils to draw lines using their rulers. Call attention to the shapes (triangles, rectangles, etc.) the intersecting lines make.

Mirror Me

Procedure: Children stand and leave at least 3 feet (.9 m) between each other. Stand facing children.

Let's pretend that I am a mirror. When you see me move, move your body the same way. Lift your arms above your head. Children move the same way. After children have mirrored your action, move again (lift one leg, bend down, touch your finger or hand to your ear, eyes, nose, hair, stomach, etc.). Trade roles with a child. Group mirrors his or her actions.

Mixing Colors

Materials: A square of red, yellow and blue cellophane for each child, white paper.

Procedure: Invite children to look through the red cellophane at different objects in the room. Then invite children to repeat with yellow and blue cellophane.

Now let's try looking through two colors at the same time. Children put red cellophane on top of yellow cellophane and look through both. **What color do you see?** Children may also lay the two squares of cellophane against the white paper. Invite children to repeat activity with other combinations of colored cellophane.

For Younger Children: Simplify activity by only inviting children to look through one color at a time.

Number Search

Materials: Large sheet of paper, marker.

Procedure: Print "1" on the paper. **What is there just one of in our classroom?** Children look around to find something in the room of which there is only one (plant, cabinet, chalkboard, door, teacher, etc.).

Print "2" on the paper. **What are there just two of in this room?** Children repeat search. Game continues as time and interest allow.

Object Order

Materials: Five of the same type of small objects (blocks, crayons, markers, figures, little books, etc.) in a variety of sizes, shapes and colors for each child.

Procedure: Give at least five objects to each child. **What is different about your blocks? Line up your blocks from the shortest to the longest.** Children line up objects according to size. Suggest other ways of lining up objects (color, shape, etc.). Suggest children trade items to accomplish a task. For example, a child with two blue crayons may trade or give one to a child who has no blue ones to complete a rainbow of colors (red, orange, yellow, green and blue).

Play Dough Shapes

Materials: Play dough; optional—plastic mats or tablecloth, small wooden rolling pins or plastic knives.

Preparation: None. (Optional: Put plastic mats or tablecloth over area where children will be working with dough.)

Procedure: Make the shape of a circle with your dough. **What shape is this? What are some things that are made of circles?** Distribute dough to each child. Children form circles. (Optional: Children use rolling pins or knives to help shape dough.) Continue with other shapes (squares, triangles, rectangles).

Pointing to Points

Procedure: Did you know we have points on our bodies? We do! Hold up your index finger and point to it. **Point to your finger the way I'm doing.** Children respond**. Your nose is a point.** Point to your nose. Continue helping children recognize other body points (shoulder, knee, elbow, etc.).

Popcorn Walk

Materials: Popped popcorn, two bowls, tablespoons.

Preparation: Fill one bowl with popped popcorn and put at one side of room. Put empty bowl at other side of room.

Procedure: Gather children near popcorn. Place several pieces of popcorn on a tablespoon. Give a child the spoon. Child walks across the room and dumps the popcorn from the spoon into the bowl. Repeat with another spoon and child. After children have had turns or when bowl is full, enjoy eating the popcorn together.

Variation: Substitute any small snack for popcorn (fish crackers, pretzels, etc.).

Quiet Touch

Procedure: Children sit or stand in a group. Choose a volunteer to go first. Volunteer silently walks to an object in the room (door, table, chalkboard, poster, etc.) and touches it. Child then returns to the group. Motion for another child to take a turn. Child walks over and touches what the first child touched and then touches another object. The game continues with each child touching in order the objects the previous children touched and then touching a new object. Children may help each other by motioning to objects in order.

Shape Search

Procedure: Children sit in a circle. Look around the room and say, **Touch your chin if you see something shaped like a square.** Children touching their chin name object shaped like a square. Repeat game with other shapes.

For Younger Children: Cut shapes from colored paper. **This is a triangle. Put your hand on your head if you see something in our room shaped like a triangle.**

For Older Children: Find five things in our room shaped like a circle and then put your hand on your knee. Repeat with other shapes.

Silent Imitation

Procedure: Children sit in a circle with you. **Without talking, watch what I do. Then do the same thing.** Touch your ears. Children touch their ears. Touch your leg. Children touch their leg. You may also hold up a number of fingers or an arm, etc.

After a few turns touching or holding up only a single body part, touch or hold up two in a row. Continue activity as children's interest allows.

For Older Children: After a few rounds, invite a child to be the leader.

Sock Game

Materials: Clean sock, several small objects.

Preparation: Put one object inside the sock and tie the top of the sock shut.

Procedure: Children sit in a circle or around a table and pass the sock around, feeling the object in the sock but not saying what they think the object is. **When you have guessed what is in the sock, don't tell.**

After everyone has had a turn, ask children to raise their hand to tell what they think is in the sock. After everyone has guessed, untie the sock and show the object. Repeat the game by secretly putting another object in the sock.

Soft, Softer, Softest

Preparation: Select a finger play or Bible verse with which children are familiar.

Procedure: Lead the children in saying the finger play or verse using motions and normal voices. Then lead the children in saying the finger play or verse in a softer voice. Then whisper the words. Finally use only the motions.

String Fun

Materials: String, scissors, blocks.

Procedure: For each child, cut a piece of string the same height as the child. Lay strings on the floor. Children line up blocks so that they are as long as the string. Then children line up blocks to be shorter or longer than the string.

Variation: Cut string as long as each child's waist is around. Child stacks blocks so that they are as long as the string and then longer or shorter than the string.

Stringing Things

Materials: Uncooked pasta in a variety of shapes and colors, lengths of string for each child.

Preparation: Tie a knot around one pasta shape at one end of each string.

Procedure: Give a string to each child. Children string pasta shapes on strings. When string is full, tie ends together. Some children may enjoy making and wearing a pasta necklace.

For Older Children: Challenge older children to create patterns with different colors and shapes of pasta.

Table Math

Materials: At least five small blocks or crayons for each child.

Procedure: Let's have fun with numbers today! Demonstrate your words. **Take one block from your pile. Put it in front of you. How many blocks are there? Now put another block beside your one block. How many blocks do you have now?** Continue with other combinations of objects to solve simple addition problems.

Variation: Challenge children with subtraction problems by having them take away objects and count the remaining ones.

Telephone

Materials: Toy telephone, bell.

Procedure: Children sit in a circle. Children pass the telephone around until you ring the bell.

The child holding the telephone when the bell rings, answers the phone by saying "Hello." Ask the child a general information question. **What is green, hops and says "ribbit"?** If necessary, give clues until the child can answer.

Start the telephone moving around the circle again, continuing the activity and using a different question for each child until all have had a turn to answer.

Too Short to Save

Materials: Marker, two index cards, masking tape, two empty boxes, basket of crayons.

Preparation: Print "Save" on one index card and "Throw Away" on the other card. Tape a card to each box. Place a strip of masking tape on the table beside where each child sits. Length of strip will be determined by the length of crayon to be saved.

Procedure: Child lays a crayon from the basket beside the strip. If the crayon is as long as the strip or longer, he or she puts the crayon in the Save box. If the crayon is shorter than the strip, he or she puts it in the Throw Away box. Continue until all crayons have been measured and put into one of the two boxes.

Commend children for their work. **I see Hannah measuring the yellow crayon very carefully. She really knows about measuring. Good work, Hannah!**

Extend the activity by providing appropriate size containers (yogurt cups, one-cup milk cartons with top removed and thoroughly rinsed, etc.) for children to separate crayons by color, one color per container.

Trace the Shape

Materials: Cardboard cut into a variety of shapes, pencils, paper, scissors.

Procedure: Give each child a cardboard shape, a pencil and sheet of paper. Children trace their shape on paper and cut it out. Children trade patterns and repeat as time and interest allow.

Under the Table Hot Potato

Materials: Beanbag, small ball or other hand-sized item; children's music cassette/ CD and player.

Procedure: Seat children at a table. Give one child the beanbag or other item. Children put their hands under the table in a position so that they can easily reach their neighbor's hands.

When the music is playing, pass the beanbag to the person sitting next to you. Demonstrate your directions. **Keep passing it around the table until the music stops. Try to pass it quietly because when the music stops, I will try to guess who has the beanbag!**

Children pass object under the table as the music plays. When music stops, take one guess as to who has the object. If you guess incorrectly, play again. If you guess correctly, invite the child who had the object to help you play the music for the next round. Repeat game as time and interest allow.

Where's the Pair?

Materials: Small index cards, a variety of stickers.

Procedure: Give each child two index cards and two matching stickers. Children place a sticker on each card. Collect one card from each child. Shuffle cards. Place the cards face down in the center of the table. Each child takes a turn to pick a card from the pile and see if the sticker on it matches the one on his or her card. Child keeps the matching card. If the card does not match, child returns it to the pile. Next child picks a card to see if it matches and the game continues in the same manner.

Who's Talking?

Procedure: Demonstrate several different voices: high, low, whisper, voice with accent, etc. Children practice talking in different ways.

Choose a sentence for the children to say (Bible verse, line from a song or other phrase). Invite a volunteer to cover his or her eyes and be the Listener. Silently choose a child to be the Talker. Talker walks behind the Listener and speaks in a disguised voice. Listener guesses who is talking. Listener selects the next child to be the Listener.

Transition Activities

Children are not always ready to move from one activity to another when the schedule says it's time. Transition activities help with those changes. They assist in bringing conclusion to a previous activity and they make the first step in moving to the next one.

Air Travel

Procedure: When children are lined up to go outside or to another room, announce, **Let's pretend we're flying in an airplane to go outside today.** Lead children to put arms out and "fly" outside, making airplane noises.

Variations: Have children imitate paddling canoes, sailing in a boat, chugging like a train or riding on a roller coaster.

Back to Line

Procedure: Stand by door while children stay where they are. **Everyone walk backward to line up by the door.** Assist children in knowing where to move to form a line.

For Younger Children: Call the names of a few children at a time to walk backward to the line.

For Older Children: Children stay with their backs toward you and walk backward to the next activity.

Caterpillar, Butterfly

Procedure: When children are lined up to go outside, say, **Put your hands on the shoulders of the person in front of you. As we walk, keep your hands on their shoulders. We'll pretend we're one great big caterpillar.**

When you are outside, announce **When caterpillars grow up, they become butterflies! Now let's act like butterflies!** Children "fly" away to enjoy their time outside.

Circus Parade

Procedure: Let's be in a circus parade! Ask a volunteer to be the Ringmaster and lead the parade line. Other children may be clowns skipping along, horses prancing, lions roaring, tigers growling, elephants trumpeting, tightrope walkers walking, etc. The Ringmaster leads the circus parade to the next location.

Clap Your Hands

Procedure: Quiet children for a story or listening time using this rhyme and actions words suggest:

I clap my hands, I touch my feet,
I jump up from the ground.
I clap my hands, I touch my feet
And turn myself around.

I clap my hands, I touch my feet,
I sit myself right down.
I clap my hands, I touch my feet,
I do not make a sound.

Clothes Call

Procedure: Invite children to line up according to clothing color to be dismissed to go to the next activity.

Sing these words to the tune of "Head, Shoulders, Knees and Toes."

Children wearing blue,
stand up, stand up.
Children wearing blue,
stand up.
Children wearing blue,
stand up.
Please line up by the
door, by the door.

Repeat with other colors until all children are in line.

Variation: In the song, include patterns on clothing (polka dots, flowers, lettering on clothes, etc.) and different areas to move to (blocks, art table, bookshelf, etc.).

Color Clues

Procedure: Ask a few children at a time to listen for a certain color in order to get in line or be excused to go to another activity. **David, Reed and Gracie, think of the color of a fire truck. When I say the right color, you may go to the puzzle table: brown, green, pink, red.**

Repeat with other children and other colored objects (sun, grass, sky, ocean, etc.).

Color Song

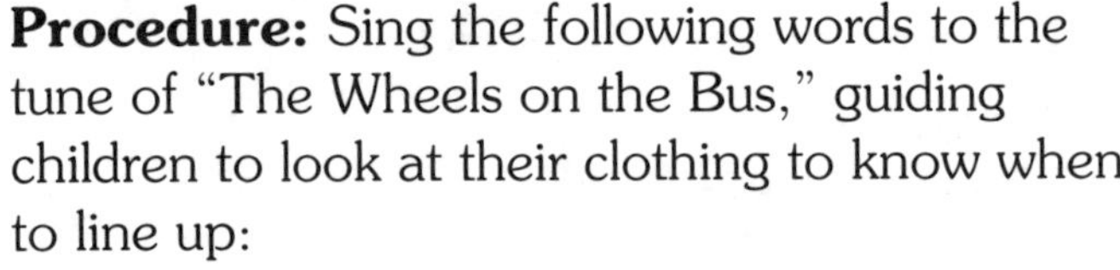

Procedure: Sing the following words to the tune of "The Wheels on the Bus," guiding children to look at their clothing to know when to line up:

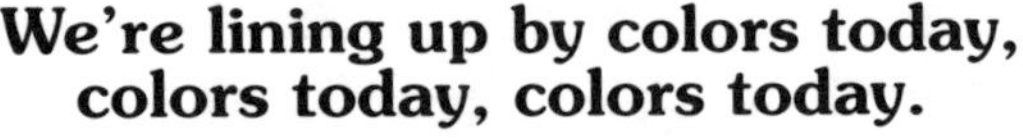

We're lining up by colors today,
colors today, colors today.

We're lining up by colors today.
Listen for your color.

If you're wearing green today, green
today, green today,

If you're wearing green today, you
may get in line.

Repeat song, naming a different color each round until all children have lined up.

Countdown

Procedure: Randomly assign each child a number. Then call out numbers in descending order. Children get in line when their number is called. Lead line to next location.

Friend Fun

Procedure: Choose one child to begin the line at the door. That child chooses a friend to line up behind him or her. The child chosen to join the line does so and then that child chooses someone to line up behind him or her. Repeat until the entire class is in line.

Getting Together

Procedure: Sing the following words to the tune of "Row, Row, Row Your Boat" and lead children in motions:

Clap, clap, clap your hands. *(Clap hands.)*
Stomp, stomp your feet. *(Stomp feet.)*
Give yourself a great big hug, *(Cross arms to hug self.)*
Because you are so neat!

Clap, clap, clap your hands. *(Clap hands.)*
Stomp, stomp your feet. *(Stomp feet.)*
Give yourself a great big hug *(Cross arms to hug self.)*
And then you take a seat. *(Sit down.)*

Hand Jive

Procedure: To gather children for the next activity, sit in the area where you want children to join you. **Come and play this game with me.** Repeat the following rhyme several times, using the actions words suggest:

One, two, three,
Hands up like me. *(Raise your hands above your head.)*

After children join you in holding their hands above their heads, repeat the rhyme, substituting the following phrases for "Hands up":

1. **Clap your hands,**
2. **Hug your chest**
3. **Pat your head**
4. **Roll your fists**
5. **Wiggle your fingers.**

Have a Seat

Procedure: Use the following rhyme to help children get seated:

> **Everybody have a seat, have a seat, have a seat.**
> **Everybody have a seat on the floor.**
> **Not on the ceiling, not on the door—**
> **Everybody have a seat on the floor.**

Here We Are!

Procedure: Children sit in a circle on the floor. Say the following rhyme:

> **Here is our circle**
> **And here we are!**
> **Here's Jenna and Heather.**
> **Here's Trevor and Logan.**

Continue to insert children's names until all have been named and then finish the rhyme:

> **And here I am, too.**
> **We're glad we're together!**
> **I'm glad I'm with you!**

Howdy, Neighbor

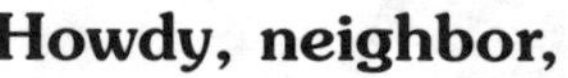

Procedure: Lead children in the following rhyme and actions to help children get seated:

Howdy, neighbor,
(Wave.)
What do you say?
(Shake hands with each other.)
It's going to be a beautiful day.
(Draw a sun with your finger.)
So clap your hands,
(Clap hands.)
And stamp your feet,
(Stamp feet.)
Jump up and down,
(Jump with two feet.)
And take your seat.
(Children sit down in a circle.)

Repeat the rhyme and actions until all children are seated.

I'll Touch

Procedure: Lead children in this stretching activity when they need a break from sitting still. Use actions words suggest.

I'll touch my head, my knee, my hand.
I'll sit up straight and then I'll stand.

I'll touch my ears, my nose, my chin,
Then quietly sit down again.

Mr. Puppet

Materials: Hand puppet.

Procedure: Use the puppet to announce the next activity to the children, give directions to come to the circle, explain activity choices or direct children to line up.

Musical Invitation

Materials: Music box.

Procedure: Play the music box as a signal to come to the circle, to begin clean up activity, to line up, etc.

Musical Parade

Procedure: What are some musical instruments people might play in a parade? Children choose an instrument to "play." Form a line and parade around the room, each child pretending to play an instrument (flute, drum, trumpet, cymbals, etc.), making the instrument's sound with their voices. Lead parade to the location to which you want children to go (outdoors, story corner, music area, etc.).

One Big Mirror

Procedure: When children are waiting in line, stand where all the children can see you. **You are going to act like my mirror. Copy my actions, like I would see in a big mirror.**

Slowly move your hands above your head. Children imitate you. Put your hands down and stick one foot out in front of you. Children copy your position. Continue doing different motions and allowing children to mirror you.

One, Two, Three–Do It!

Procedure: Lead children to say the following rhyme, using actions words suggest:

Stand up and turn around. One, two, three.
Now bend and touch your toes. One, two, three.
Reach very, very high. One, two, three.
Now flap your wings and try to fly. One, two, three.
Now sit down quietly. One, two, three.

Variation: Bring a calendar or magazine picture. Add a last line: **Here is a picture for you to see! One, two, three.**

The Pointing Game

Procedure: Lead children in the following rhyme and actions words indicate to get children's attention:

Point to the window, point to the door.
Point to the ceiling, point to the floor.
Point to the table, point to the chair.
Point to a friend who's sitting right there.
Point to your elbow, point to your knee.
Point to your foot, now point to ME!

Rap Call

Procedure: Use the following rhyme and motions to gather children together. Begin by snapping your fingers or clapping your hands.

If you want to hear a story,
This is what you do.
You sit right down
Like the other kids do.
You listen to your teacher
And you raise your hand real high.
That's right, *(Snap finger and point to a child who is sitting down with hand raised. Child then puts hand down.)*
That's right, *(Point to next child who is sitting down with hand raised.)*
That's right. *(Point to next child who is sitting down with hand raised.)*

Continue until all children are seated.

Sticker Search

Materials: Index cards, four or five copies of a sticker for each activity center you have available.

Preparation: Put each sticker on a separate index card. Place one card at each activity center.

Procedure: Give an index card to each child. **Look at the sticker on the card I gave you. Find the card with the sticker that matches yours at one of our activity centers. You get to go to that activity center today.**

Variation: Draw shapes instead of using stickers.

Story Setting

Procedure: Before a story or other listening activity, lead children in the following rhyme and actions:

Sometimes my hands are at my side;
(Place hands by hips.)

Then behind my back they will hide.
(Put hands behind back.)

Sometimes I wiggle my fingers so,
(Wiggle fingers.)

Shake them fast, shake them slow!
(Shake hands quickly and then slowly.)

Sometimes my hands go clap, clap, clap;
(Clap hands.)

Then I rest them in my lap.
(Put hands in lap.)

Now they're quiet as can be,
(Put finger to lips for "Shh.")

Because it's story time, you see.

Time to Go

Procedure: Sing the following words to the tune of "The Farmer in the Dell" as a signal for children to get ready to move to another location:

It's time to go outside.
It's time to go outside.
Everybody to the door,
It's time to go outside.

Variation: Challenge children to sing the song several times with you. Vary ways of singing (loudly, softly, clap rhythmically, etc.).

Tiptoe Trails

Procedure: Stand by the door. **Everyone tiptoe here to line up by me.** Ask volunteers to lead the line on a "tiptoe trail" as children move to a new location.

For Younger Children: Lead children in tiptoeing as you say the following rhyme:

Let's all tiptoe to the playground,
Tiptoe after me.
Let's all tiptoe to the playground,
And see how quiet we can be.

Travel This Way

Procedure: When children are lining up, ask a volunteer, **What way would you like to travel today?** If a child needs help thinking of ideas, suggest march like a band, skate like an ice-skater, swim like a dolphin, glide like a skier, etc. Lead the line of children to move as suggested to the next activity or location.

For Younger Children: Tell children a way to move (skip, hop, walk heel-toe, tiptoe, etc.), rather than asking a volunteer for a suggestion.

Watch Carefully!

Procedure: When children are sitting in a group getting ready to move to another location, begin clapping your hands slowly and say to the beat of your clapping, **Watch my hands because they just might change!**

When you see my hands change what they are doing, raise your hand. Change your hands to another motion (tapping your knees, head, chest, shoulders or ears; clapping two fingers together; snapping your fingers; rubbing your legs or forearms). Dismiss a few children at a time who have raised their hand when they noticed you changing motions. Continue activity until all children have been dismissed.

What Do You Want to Do?

Procedure: Children sit in a circle. Sing the following words to the tune of "London Bridge Is Falling Down" to ask children what specific activity they want to do next:

Do you want to play with blocks,
Play with blocks, play with blocks?
If you want to play with blocks,
Raise your hand.

Dismiss children with raised hands to the block area.

Repeat song with the other activities (cut and color, clean the house, play with puzzles, work with dough, etc.).

Where Am I?

Procedure: When children need to move to another area or be dismissed to go home, give clues to children according to their location. **If you are sitting at the puzzle table, you may get your jacket. If you are sitting between Henry and Sam, you may get your work from the table. If you are sitting next to Alicia, you may move to the book corner.** Continue until all children have been given an instruction.

Whisper Words

Procedure: I'm going to talk very quietly. Listen closely. Whisper, **When you hear me say your name, you may go sit at the snack table.** Whisper each child's name until all children have moved to the next activity.

Variation: Silently mouth the child's name.

For Younger Children: Introduce the activity, **Look at me and be very quiet, so you can hear me when I call your name.**

For Older Children: Whisper each child's name and include directions. **Juan, skip to the puzzle table. Sam, slide your feet slowly to the art table.**

Yes and No!

Materials: Red and green construction paper, marker, scissors.

Preparation: Print "NO" on the red construction paper and "YES" on the green construction paper.

Procedure: While children are gathering for circle time, announce, **When I hold up this green Yes sign, everyone may keep talking and moving around to find a seat. When I hold up this red No sign, everyone needs to stop talking and sit down.**

Hold up Yes and No signs several times. End the activity by holding up the No sign.

Word Activities

for Older Children

Take advantage of children's interest in learning to read by leading them in a variety of language activities. Written especially for older children, word activities encourage children to practice and expand their vocabulary.

Add-On Thanks

Procedure: Children sit in a circle. **I'm thankful for cheese.** Each child takes a turn adding on another food for which he or she is thankful. Child tries to repeat all the foods already said, before adding the name of his or her food. Begin the activity again when the number of foods reaches five.

If time and interest allow, repeat the activity using the names of nature items, animals, etc.

Add-On Words

Procedure: Children sit in a circle on floor. Begin game by saying a simple sentence. **Here is my cat.** Each child takes a turn to add on a descriptive word about the cat, after repeating descriptions already said. ("My cat is black." "My cat is black and little." "My cat is black and little and likes milk.") Begin activity again when number of descriptive words reaches five.

Alphabet Activity

Procedure: What letter comes after the letter *A*? Volunteers respond. The child who answers suggests a new letter.

Variation: If the children in your group are unsure of the sequence of alphabet letters, display an alphabet line to which they may refer. Or use the names of the days of the week in place of alphabet letters.

Animal Rhymes

Procedure: Begin activity by saying the first part of a rhyming sentence, such as, **Up in a tree, I see a . . . What is an animal that rhymes with tree?** Child completes sentence with an animal or insect that rhymes with "tree" (bee).

Jumping on the log, I see a (frog).

Hiding in the house, I see a (mouse).

Chewing on my coat, I see a (goat).

Chasing the rat, I see a (cat).

Scooting under the rug, I see a (bug).

Swimming in a dish, I see a (fish).

Walking in the pen, I see a (hen).

Sitting there so big, I see a (pig).

Crawling on a plant, I see an (ant).

Category Callout

Procedure: Name two colors. Volunteers name two specific colors.

Repeat activity, substituting each of the following categories: stores, fruits, vegetables, toys, songs, places, etc. Add categories or vary the number of items to name within that category as time and interest allow.

Creation List

Preparation: Large sheet of paper, marker.

Procedure: Ask children to name animals for each letter of the alphabet (anteater, bear, cow, dog, etc.). Print names on paper. Challenge children to name enough animals to fill the entire paper.

Grandma's House

Procedure: Sit in a circle with children. **I packed my bag to go to Grandma's and I took a sweater.** Next child repeats your entire sentence and adds an item ("I packed my bag to go to Grandma's and I took a sweater and a ball.") Next child repeats the sentence with previous items and adds one of his or her own. Each child repeats and adds one item until the number of objects reaches five. Then begin the game again.

For Older Children: Challenge older children to be play the game alphabetically, so each item added to the list begins with the next letter of the alphabet.

Group Scoop

Procedure: Raise your hand when you hear a word that doesn't belong: turtle, cow, cat, grape, dog.

After children have identified that "grape" doesn't belong, ask, **Why doesn't grape belong? What are the other things I named?** (Animals.) Repeat with other categories (foods, colors, shapes, boy's names, girl's names, etc.).

For Younger Children: Collect pictures of animals, foods, colors and shapes. On the floor or table, place pictures from one category plus one picture from another category. Children name the contents of each picture to determine which picture does not belong.

Heard the Word

Procedure: Raise your hand when you hear a word that rhymes with "head": car, ant, red, toy.

After children have identified "red," repeat with a new beginning word and a set of words, one of which rhymes with the beginning word.

Listen Up!

Procedure: Think of an object familiar to children. Tell clues so that the children can guess the object. **I'm thinking of something red. It grows on trees. We can eat it. It has seeds.** After each clue, pause for children to guess object. Allow the child who correctly guesses the object to think of the next object and give clues for group to guess.

Repeat activity with another object. Continue as time and interest allow.

Opposites

Procedure: Say a word and ask children to name the opposite word.

hot—cold
up—down
black—white
young—old
short—tall
day—night
big—little
sit—stand
stop—go
open—close
top—bottom
left—right
sad—happy
frown—smile
asleep—awake
over—under
shout—whisper

Partner Words

Procedure: Say a word and invite children to name a word that is associated with that word.

salt—pepper
shoes—socks, laces, slippers
spoon—fork, bowl, knife
pencil—paper, pen, eraser
bread—butter, jam, toast
coat—hat, mittens, boots

Rhyme Time

Procedure: Say a one-syllable word and invite children to tell rhyming words.

hid—bid, lid, grid, kid, did, mid, rid
game—aim, blame, came, fame, lame, name, same, tame
old—bold, cold, fold, gold, hold, mold, sold, told
go—bow, blow, Joe, know, low, mow, sew, toe, woe
bat—cat, sat, mat, at, pat

Starts with S

Procedure: Let's say as many words as we can that begin with the letter *S*. Children take turns saying any words that start with an *S* sound. When children have run out of ideas for one letter, repeat with another letter.

What If?

Materials: Paper-towel tube or capped marker for pretend microphone.

Procedure: Children sit in a circle. Interview a child, asking into the microphone, **If you were an animal, what kind would you be?** Give the microphone to the child for him or her to use when answering.

Repeat until all children have had a turn. Use the same question for each child, or substitute any of the following questions:

1. **If you had to be something green, what would you be?**
2. **If you were given lots of money, what would you buy?**
3. **If you were a giant dinosaur, what would you do?**
4. **If you were the teacher, what would you do?**
5. **If you could be any age you wanted, how old would you be? Why?**

Variation: Use a tape recorder to record children's responses. Then play the tape for children to hear and identify the speaker.

What's Bigger?

Procedure: When I name something, you tell me something that is bigger than that object. Nickel—shoe, car, quarter, doll, house, etc. Give each child an opportunity to name something.

Repeat activity, naming other objects (a pencil, a ladybug, an ant, a butterfly, a swimming pool, a sock, etc.). Children continue naming objects bigger than the one you named.

Variation: When I name something, tell me something that is smaller than that object. Name items such as a car, crayon, bus, watch, banana, basketball, etc.

What's Next?

Materials: 26 sheets of paper, marker.

Preparation: Print a capital letter of the alphabet on the 26 sheets of paper, one letter on each sheet.

Procedure: Children stand in a line or sit in a circle. Give each child one or two pieces of paper. **Who has the first letter of the alphabet?** That child places the *A* paper on the floor; then ask, **What's next?** Child with *B* places his or her paper beside the *A*. Continue until the alphabet is complete.

Variation: Mature learners will enjoy beginning with the letter *Z* and placing the letters in the reverse order.